"*Time to Talk* is a phenomenally valuable and highly readable guide to your child's speech and language development. I wish this book had been available when my children were babies. Dr. Michelle and Carlyn have distilled a vast academic literature down into a single volume full of clear explanations, illustrative stories, and practical tips that will be helpful to all parents who want to enrich their children's learning environments. Parents of children with delays or other special needs will find the authors' clear and honest introduction to speech and language services to be especially useful. "

> —Margo Gardner, Ph.D., Senior Research Scientist,
> National Center for Children and Families,
> Teachers College, Columbia University

"From tips to takeaways to red flags to Q&As, Dr. Michelle has created an in-depth treasure book of priceless information that can be easily digested by busy parents and education professionals."

> —Sarita Austin, Ph.D., CCC-SLP, TSHH, Cert HCPC, MRCSLT,
> Director, Department of Speech-Language Pathology, New York
> Center for Child Development, Founder and Artistic Director
> www.pureflowtheatreworks.com

"While giving a lucid and clear introduction to the building blocks of speech and language including hearing, where this book really shines is in making clear the milestones that should be reached in a child with normally developing speech and language. If an evaluation or therapy is necessary, this knowledge will prevent any delays that could adversely affect the child. A remarkable feat."

> —Ari J Goldsmith, MD, FAAP, Pediatric Otolaryngology
> (Ear, Nose and Throat), Maimonides Pediatric
> Otolaryngology, Brooklyn, New York

Time to Talk

Time to Talk

What You Need to Know About Your Child's
Speech and Language Development

MICHELLE MACROY-HIGGINS Ph.D.

CARLYN KOLKER

NEW YORK

Bulk discounts available. For details visit:
www.amacombooks.org/go/specialsales
Or contact special sales:
Phone: 800-250-5308
Email: specialsls@amanet.org
View all the AMACOM titles at: www.amacombooks.org

American Management Association: *www.amanet.org*

Library of Congress Cataloging-in-Publication Data

Names: MacRoy-Higgins, Michelle, author. | Kolker, Carlyn, author.
Title: Time to talk : what you need to know about your child's speech and
    language development / Michelle MacRoy-Higgins, Ph.D. and Carlyn Kolker.
Description: New York, NY : AMACOM, a division of American Management
    Association, [2017] | Includes index.
Identifiers: LCCN 2016042385 (print) | LCCN 2016054186 (ebook) | ISBN
    9780814437292 (pbk.) | ISBN 9780814437308 (eBook)
Subjects: LCSH: Children--Language. | Verbal ability in children. | Language
    awareness in children. | Child development. | Language acquisition.
Classification: LCC LB1139.L3 M23 2017 (print) | LCC LB1139.L3 (ebook) | DDC
    372.6--dc23
LC record available at https://lccn.loc.gov/2016042385

ACKNOWLEDGMENTS

Thank you to so many friends, colleagues, and family members who helped us create *Time to Talk*.

An enormous thank-you to all the families who have shared their stories with us, especially those we interviewed for our A Parent's Perspective feature. Everything we learned from you is a part of this book.

A few people deserve a special shout-out:

Thank you to Dr. Michael Higgins, who was *all ears* throughout the entire process of writing this manuscript, and especially for his contributions to Chapters 1 and 7.

Dr. Nancy Eng shared her expertise in multilingualism both as a professional and as a parent.

Meg Moorhouse helped us realize *Time to Talk* from a sloppy few scraps of paper to a truly professional act.

Abigail Koons believed in our vision and stuck with us. Thank you to Abby and everyone at Park Literary for your help, patience, and guidance.

We were so extremely lucky to work with Bob Nirkind, a gifted, swift, and exacting editor who was always a joy to collaborate and correspond with.

Aimee Sicuro gave us the best drawing of an ear a human could make.

Thank you to those who read, commented on, and provided advice on our proposal and manuscript, including Natalie Buzzeo, Paul Cascella, Helen Coster, Kevin Dalton, Dana Dillon, Elizabeth Galletta, Elizabeth Gradinger, Gabrielle Kahn, Abigail Marcus, Antonia Schroeder, Craig Selinger, Amy Singer, Sara Weiss, and Lauren Zierer.

ACKNOWLEDGMENTS

Research related to this manuscript was supported by Hunter College of the City University of New York (CUNY) through PSC-CUNY Grant 67710-00 45 and the President's Fund for Faculty Advancement.

And finally to our families, who put up with us during many nights of talking and writing and especially Annabel, Caleb, Charlotte, and Zeke—our very own talkers.

CONTENTS

CONTENTS

Time to Talk

INTRODUCTION

I N THE BOOK you're now holding in your hands, we're going to look closely at how your child learns to talk. The process is sometimes magical, sometimes tedious, sometimes frustrating, sometimes hilarious, sometimes easy, and sometimes difficult.

Our goal in *Time to Talk* is simple: to demystify how your child learns to communicate with the world. Your child's speech and language development begins the moment she is born and yelps her first cry, and unfolds throughout her childhood. Talking is the starting point for conveying ideas, expressing needs and wants, interacting with others, and even learning to read.

The more you understand how your child begins to communicate, the more you can be there for him. When it comes to childhood development, knowledge is not just power but also *empowerment*: If you know how your child learns to talk, then you can help him talk more. You can help him listen better. You can help him improve his interactions with peers and teachers, friends and family. Eventually, you can help him progress from mastering the spoken word to conquering the written word. And you can be on the lookout for signs of challenges and difficulties, know when to seek help, and, if help is necessary, understand what therapy your child may need and how to get it for him.

THE ORGANIZATION AND CONTENTS OF THIS BOOK

Speech and language development require lots of tools. These tools are physical, cognitive, social, and emotional. Some of them are innate, such as moving your mouth, and others are learned, such as grasping the meaning of a new vocabulary word. In this book, we explain how your child acquires each of these tools to create the complete set she needs.

We have organized our book to, first, familiarize you with these tools of communication: hearing, speech, language, fluency, and literacy. Then we take a deeper look at questions you may have about how your child acquires his talking tool set. The first five chapters are dedicated to providing a practical, insightful look at the essential components of listening, speaking, and reading. The sixth chapter follows up by explaining how these components come into play for children exposed to multiple languages. And finally, the last two chapters address particular concerns you may have regarding your child's speech and language development. Here, we discuss specific challenges and impairments that some children face, and we review the numerous options available to seek help for your child.

Let's get started by touching on each topic in a little more detail. Chapter 1 focuses on hearing, because good hearing lays the fundamental groundwork for spoken language. This discussion covers everything from how hearing development happens, to the anatomy and physiology of the ear, to the types of hearing loss, and more.

In Chapter 2 we move on to address the critical subject of speech development, the process that begins with your baby's first cries and continues as your toddler babbles and your child learns to say new sounds and words. Here we look at what speech development means, how and when children acquire new sounds, and when children typically begin to achieve clarity in their speech.

Chapter 3 explores language development. We explain the common rules and conventions of language, discuss how children pick up new words, look at when they begin to use words to express their needs and wants, and describe how young children are simultaneously able to understand and utter language. We also investigate why some children begin to talk a little bit later than others.

Chapter 4 covers the concept of fluency, the ability to talk easily and smoothly. Because fluency is an important aspect of communicating with others, we look at why some kids master this skill seemingly without effort while others sometimes need extra time and help.

Because oral language and written language are so closely intertwined, in Chapter 5 we explain how early literacy unfolds. We explore the first steps that children take in recognizing letters and the sounds they make, discuss how to build critical early literacy skills from the youngest age, and give you some great suggestions about how to introduce a love of reading to your child.

In Chapter 6 we focus on how some young children are able to acquire not just one language, but multiple languages—all when they're still in diapers! We distinguish among the different forms of and approaches to bilingualism, and offer some advice about how to raise your child bilingually either at home, at school, or both.

Finally, we turn to special concerns that may arise for you and your children when your kids learn to talk. In Chapter 7, we discuss particular communication disorders and difficulties that can affect your child's ability to talk or listen, and others that may make it harder for her to excel in a school setting. We also give you some of the defining characteristics of these challenges and disorders so that you can spot them.

We know that all this information can lead to lots of questions about how to get help for your child if you think she needs it, so in Chapter 8 we explain the complex systems of help that you may have to navigate if your child needs some extra assistance in her mastery of talking. We cover the different kinds of professionals you might want to visit, the different systems that are available to you—both public and private—to receive therapy, and an array of therapy options for your child. Because these systems can sometimes be hard to pursue, our goal is to make it easy for you to find help for your child.

In the first six chapters of this book, we explain how and when typically developing children acquire different skills and abilities, and then we provide you with actionable advice about how to help your child grow, how to spot difficulties and challenges, and when it may be necessary to seek experts. This advice is presented in several special sections: **Red Flags: What to Look Out For and When**, are tips on any cause for concern; **Common Questions, Expert Answers** are those questions that parents frequently ask about each topic, with easy-to-read responses; and **Some Simple Things to Do at Home** are suggestions for nurturing your child's communication skills. Additionally, each chapter ends with a **Resources** section that provides you with extra online information to consult.

Throughout the book you'll also find a number of other features that are both helpful and informative: You may find a **Parenting Tip** on how you can help your child at home. **From Research to Real Life** is a plain-English summary of relevant scientific research. We also present **A Parent's Perspective**, where we introduce you to parents who have faced challenges and overcome them.

We are parents too. We know what it is like to try to "research" your child's development. There are the stealth observations of other people's children on the playground, not to mention the late-night Google sessions. But those aren't sound scientific ways to learn about how your child is growing. Our book represents a different choice: one grounded in academic research but written for everyday parents. There's no jargon. We define scientific and medical terms so you can understand them. *Time to Talk* is meant to be your guidebook—not your textbook.

INTRODUCING THE AUTHORS

We have created the winning combination of sound research and plain-English prose because we have a winning team of authors—a PhD (who is a parent) and a writer (who is a parent).

Dr. Michelle MacRoy-Higgins—or simply Dr. Michelle—is an associate professor in the Department of Speech-Language Pathology and Audiology at Hunter College in New York City. She has a BS and MS in speech-language pathology and a PhD in speech-language-hearing sciences. She has her Certificate of Clinical Competence (CCC) from the American Speech-Language-Hearing Association (ASHA), is licensed in New York State as a speech-language pathologist—also called a speech therapist or a speech language therapist, which is the term we'll use in this book—and has worked as a classroom teacher. Dr. Michelle has evaluated and worked with hundreds of children ages 6 months to 10 years with their speech and language issues. She has worked as a speech language therapist in preschools, elementary schools, university clinics, on a Native American reservation, and in children's homes.

Dr. Michelle is married to an audiologist, someone who studies and tests kids' hearing; we'll call him Dr. Mike. Together, they are raising two young girls, so Dr. Michelle has had a lot of personal experience observing kids learning to talk. In other words, when it comes to speech and language, she has pretty much seen and heard it all!

Dr. Michelle's partner in this venture, Carlyn Kolker, is a writer who is raising two boys. Carlyn has written about legal and business topics for more than 15 years, and has a knack for turning complicated scientific terms and other mumbo-jumbo into readable material.

TIME TO TALK'S ORIGIN STORY

Time to Talk is a parenting book formed during the early days of the authors' own parenting journeys. Several years ago, Dr. Michelle and Carlyn lived in the same apartment building in Brooklyn, New York. Their second children were born just a few weeks apart, and they spent many hours of their maternity leaves home together, swapping stories of sleep deprivation and feeding woes. Somehow, while their babies wailed and their toddlers flung toys at each other, they managed to talk about their life goals. Dr. Michelle said that, as a professor and a practicing speech language therapist, not a day went by when parents didn't have a question for her about their child's speech and language development. She confessed that she always wanted to write a book to address all of these queries. But she was looking for someone to help her write it. As it happens, Carlyn said she had always been fascinated by childhood development, and as a professional writer she was really itching to write a book—she just needed a topic!

And so, just as their youngest kids began to say their first words, Dr. Michelle and Carlyn started writing down the first words of what would eventually become this book. And we hope that as your child gets ready to say his first words or begins to utter new words that you, too, will make some time for *Time to Talk*.

1

HEARING

A Building Block to Talking

F OR YOUR CHILD to speak and communicate verbally, she needs a few things in place—like hearing. Hearing is one of the most important building blocks for effective oral communication. To most of us, it is absolutely effortless. Unlike talking, which develops over years through a series of changes, hearing begins to develop in the womb. It is part of an incredibly complex system that involves tiny bones and cells in the ear and neural pathways to the brain, and if your child's auditory system is not working fully, many of her communication abilities can be compromised.

Difficulty hearing can have an impact on social interaction and academic performance in children. Good hearing brings about timely speech and language development—everything from mastering correct pronunciation to learning proper grammar to laying the groundwork for reading. Your child's ability to hear can have a profound effect on his listening comprehension and his behavior. This includes being able to follow directions and pay attention to the teacher in school.

Parents have a lot to look out for in terms of kids' hearing issues. According to the National Institutes of Health, between two and three kids of every 1,000 children are born either deaf or with a hearing loss.

And hearing issues can lurk even when you do not expect them: More than 90 percent of deaf babies are born to hearing parents.

In addition, some kids develop hearing loss as they get older. According to the American Speech-Language-Hearing Association, two in every 100 children have experienced some sort of hearing loss. Children may get ear infections, suffer accidents, or lose some hearing as a result of a separate underlying health condition.

But the good news is that medical advances have made it far easier for parents to address their child's hearing needs. We have more and better tools to detect hearing loss at even the earliest stages of life. And we have great methods to ensure that our babies and toddlers can truly hear us, even if it seems like they are always tuning us out. In addition, parents also have a range of corrective devices, therapies, and surgeries available to them.

In this chapter, we will help empower all parents to understand if their child suffers hearing loss—with the goal of making sure their kids are great communicators.

WHAT'S HEARING, ANYWAY?

Hearing, simply defined, is the ability to detect sound. **Sound** is the occurrence of vibration of air particles. For a person or a thing to make a sound, a particular event must occur, like using your vocal cords or plucking strings on a guitar. This, in turn, causes tiny air particles to vibrate. Sounds can be emitted at different **frequencies**, the rate at which vibration occurs over a period of time, depending on how big the vibrating object is. We interpret frequency as the highness or lowness of the sound, or **pitch**. For example, men's vocal cords vibrate slower than women's vocal cords because they are bigger, and men's voices typically have a lower pitch in comparison to women's voices.

The frequency of sound is measured in **hertz** (Hz). We can perceive sounds ranging from 20 Hz (very low frequency sounds like those made by a pipe organ) to 20,000 Hz (very high frequency sounds like the buzz from a mosquito). When we speak, we emit sounds that are high, middle, and low frequency—even in the space of one sentence. You might not realize it, but when you utter a few simple words like *My name is Sarah*, you are speaking in frequencies as low as 100 Hz and as high as 12,000 Hz. Your child needs to be able to perceive a variation of frequencies to adequately hear important differences in speech sounds.

The intensity of sound is measured in **decibels** (dB). Most people can hear very quiet sounds, like whispering, which tends to clock in at around 20 to 30 dB, and feel pain when hearing very loud sounds like a jackhammer, which is usually at about 130 to 140 dB. People who cannot hear sounds at 90 dB or greater are considered to have a profound hearing loss; in other words, they are considered to be **deaf**.

Hearing is different from listening, although the two words seem almost like twins. **Listening** refers to our ability to pay attention to and interpret sound. When our ears pay attention to and interpret the acoustic information around us—such as how loud or fast a vibration is—we can actually extract meaning from the sound. For example, we know when we hear a siren that an ambulance or a fire truck is nearby, or when a baby cries that she is hungry or distressed.

We use both of our ears to know the direction in which sound is coming from. This ability is called **localization** or **directional hearing**. Hearing loss in one ear can negatively affect that ability, especially in noisy environments like classrooms or playgrounds. Not knowing where sound is coming from can have a negative impact on listening and learning as kids can have trouble focusing on important acoustics (such as their teacher's voice) and blocking out background noise.

Some kids can't detect the range of frequencies that others can; other kids can't perceive sound at quiet levels; and yet others can't localize sound. Our ability to perceive sound and to give meaning to it are the essential ingredients for your child to gain the speech and language skills she will need.

OUR NOISY WORLD

WE LIVE IN a noisy world. We are exposed to noise all day long. Some of this noise is potentially harmful to your child's hearing and, of course, your own. Later in this chapter, we'll walk you through the physical damage that noise can do to your child's ear. But before we get there, we want to introduce some facts about the world your child lives in and how modern technology may be harming your child in ways you may never have considered.

According to the American Speech-Language-Hearing Association (ASHA), sounds that are louder than 85 decibels—such as a blow dryer, a kitchen blender, a lawn mower, or a nearby subway or bus—can cause permanent hearing loss. Noises that your child may be exposed to every day can all exceed this recommended level.

There are other sound demons that are probably right in your living room. Your TV can be well over 85 dB, too. Does your child ever use your phone or a tablet to watch cartoons or play games? Guess what? If the volume is on high and the device is close to your child's ears, it may be exceeding ASHA's recommended sound level. Some toy phones, music players, trucks, or talking dolls are also well above ASHA's recommended level for noise. Kids like to put things close to their ears—so keep the noisy toys away. (See the Resources section at the end of this chapter for a guide to consult on toys to avoid.)

HOW DOES HEARING DEVELOPMENT HAPPEN?

Your baby's ears start to form at about 3 weeks gestation, and some parts are fully formed when she hits the 20-week mark in the womb.

By that time, babies can detect sound. Remember, your baby is floating in a big bath of water, so she can't hear all the sounds that we hear every day, but certain aspects of sound, such as intonation and rhythm, are transmitted well to your baby's ears.

While your baby is in utero, growing and getting bigger, he is listening to the sounds all around him—like the noise on the street or the music in your home, as well as to the language or languages that are being spoken around him.

Research over the past 30 years by scholars such as Patricia Kuhl, Anne Fernald, and Peter Jusczyk has shown that babies must be listening because they respond to human voices in utero. By the time babies are born, they show a preference for what pediatric specialists refer to as **infant-directed speech**—or in less fancy terms, baby talk—the sing-song talk that we tend to use when we speak to babies. They can also distinguish between different speech sounds, like *p* versus *b*, and can detect their mother's voice over other female voices.

DR. MICHELLE'S TAKEAWAY

START TALKING to your baby in utero. He is listening to you! And when he's finally in your arms, don't stop talking. He's listening even more!

LET'S LOOK AT THE ANATOMY AND PHYSIOLOGY OF THE EAR

Look at your baby's ears. They are so small. But they are so, so powerful. That tiny little ear has three main parts: the outer ear, middle ear, and inner ear. Hearing is about the connection of these different parts of the ear, about the workings of the ear with the brain, and about how all these parts and pathways work together. Specialists refer to all of this as the **auditory system**, the sensory framework for hearing.

The three parts of the ear join forces with pathways to the brain to make hearing happen.

THE OUTER EAR

The **outer ear**, which includes the part of the ear that is visible on a person, brings sound from the environment to the inner parts of the ear. It consists of the **pinna**, the floppy part on the outside of your head, and the **ear canal**, the narrow tubelike passage through which sound enters the internal part of the ear. The pinna collects and directs sound to the ear canal. Sound traveling through your ear canal makes your **eardrum**, the thin elastic membrane that separates the middle ear from the outer ear, vibrate.

THE MIDDLE EAR

The **middle ear** contains the three small bones, called **ossicles**, that attach to the eardrum. When the eardrum vibrates, these bones move and carry the sound vibrations. Our middle ear contains the opening to our Eustachian tube, which connects to the back of our throat and is responsible for equalizing ear pressure. When you travel in an airplane or drive up a large hill and your ears pop, your Eustachian tube is equalizing pressure. File away the words "Eustachian tube" for later, because they are really important in child-rearing—especially if your kid ever complains of an earache.

THE INNER EAR

The **inner ear**, which is involved in both hearing and balance, contains the **cochlea**, the sensory organ of hearing that is filled with fluid. The cochlea transmits sound energy to a neurological code. As the ossicles move, they set the fluid in the cochlea into motion. The cochlea is lined with tiny hair cells that bend in response to movement of the fluid. When the hair cells bend, an electrical impulse travels from the inner ear to the **auditory nerve,** the cranial nerve responsible for sensory information.

LAST STOP: THE BRAIN

From the auditory nerve, sound travels through the **central auditory pathways,** the nerve cells and fibers that connect the auditory nerve to our brain. The brain then figures out how to interpret these sounds, knowing that, perhaps, the loud sound outside means a car is honking or those words coming out of Mommy's mouth are your cue that dinner is being served.

Figure 1-1 shows the auditory system.

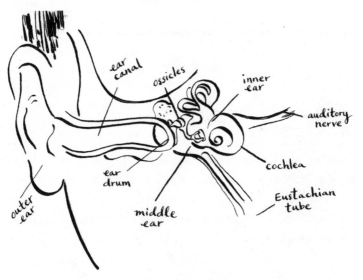

Figure 1-1. Ear diagram.

FROM RESEARCH TO REAL LIFE

HOW IS HEARING and speech perception related to speech production? Typically developing children learn speech through **audition**, the ability to hear and process sounds. Children have to hear speech sounds and detect meaningful differences in what they hear in order to say these sounds themselves. Children talk the way they hear, so if they are not hearing adequately, they will not say their speech sounds clearly. Researchers have also shown that early speech perception abilities are important for language development later on. Scholars such as April Benesish, Patricia Kuhl, and Janet Werker have shown a positive correlation between infant speech perception skills and language development in childhood.

TYPES OF HEARING LOSS

The ear is a very intricate organ, and both the ear itself and the auditory system in general can run into problems; many of these problems can lead to hearing loss. If you are concerned about your child's hearing you should visit two specialists. **Ear-nose-throat (ENT) doctors**, also called **otolaryngologists** (but usually only by other doctors), are medical specialists in—guess what—ears, noses, and throats. ENTs can interpret hearing tests, perform surgery, and prescribe medication. Some ENTs further specialize in pediatrics. **Audiologists** are hearing specialists who have advanced university degrees in audiology (the study of hearing disorders), hold a license to practice in their state, and can evaluate and treat hearing, balance, and auditory disorders. Audiologists typically perform hearing tests and dispense hearing aids and often work either in practices with ENTs or in hospitals, clinics, or schools.

If you suspect your child may have one of the hearing impairments that we are about to discuss, then run, don't walk, to your nearest ENT or audiologist. (Consult Chapter 8 for tips on finding good specialists.) **Hearing loss can be a major contributor to speech and language delays, so the faster you can address your child's hearing impairment, the faster you may be addressing his communication potential.**

Young children can face hearing impairments for two reasons:

1. Babies can be born with hearing loss. This is called **congenital hearing loss**.
2. Young children can also suffer hearing loss after birth due to infections or environmental factors. This is called **acquired hearing loss**.

Specialists divide the universe of hearing loss into two broad categories:

1. **Conductive hearing loss** is caused by an abnormality in the outer or middle ear.
2. **Sensorineural hearing loss** is caused by damage in the inner ear—to the hair cells of the cochlea or the auditory nerve.

An individual can have both conductive and sensorineural hearing loss, which is called **mixed hearing loss**.

CONDUCTIVE HEARING LOSS

Conductive hearing loss occurs when the outer or middle ear is not working properly. A rip or hole in the eardrum, buildup of wax in the ear canal, or damage to the ossicles in the middle ear will not allow sound to travel to the inner ear. The most common cause of conductive hearing loss in children is fluid in the middle ear.

DR. MICHELLE'S TAKEAWAY

THE GOOD NEWS about conductive hearing loss is that most of the time it is reversible and can be corrected with surgery or medications.

Conductive hearing loss usually causes a certain degree of hearing difficulty, but not complete deafness. Children who experience it may have difficulty hearing quiet sounds, such as whispering, or medium sounds, such as conversational speech.

Ear Infections

Guys, this is the biggie. **The single most common type of hearing loss experienced by children is caused by fluid in the middle ear, stemming from an infection.** The technical term for ear infection is **otitis media**; if your child goes to the pediatrician complaining of an earache, you're likely to come back home with the diagnosis of otitis media. Ear infections lead to a buildup of fluid in the middle ear, which in turn causes conductive hearing loss because the fluid doesn't allow the bones in the ear to vibrate properly.

Ear infections are very common in children; according to the National Institutes of Health, five out of six children experience ear infections by the time they are three years old. Young children experience ear infections more frequently than older children or adults, because the Eustachian tubes in babies and young children are shorter and more horizontal. The Eustachian tube equalizes pressure in the middle ear and drains fluid. In adults, it is sloped downward, which allows fluid to drain easily. In babies, fluid is more likely to be trapped and remain in the middle ear. As a child grows, the Eustachian tube gradually becomes sloped and the child is less likely to experience ear infections.

Because ear infections tend to occur when toddlers are developing their speech and language skills, they are important for parents to pay attention to. For some children, having an ear infection can be like listening to the world with your hands over your ears. Academic research is conflicted about the long-term impact that ear infections have on speech and language development. But we know this: Adequate hearing is needed to develop speech. And ear infections accompanied by middle ear fluid result in hearing loss.

┌─────────────── **DR. MICHELLE'S TAKEAWAY** ───────────────┐

WHILE EAR INFECTIONS themselves don't cause speech delays, even *some* hearing loss caused by fluid associated with ear infections can trigger a speech delay. Pediatricians are able to treat ear infections, but they do not typically monitor a child's hearing. So if your child is only being treated for an ear infection and his hearing is not regularly monitored, he may be experiencing undiagnosed temporary hearing loss. Your child should visit an ENT if he experiences repeated ear infections or if you suspect hearing loss.

└──┘

Ear infections come in many different shapes and sizes.

▶ ACUTE OTITIS MEDIA

The "acute" in front of the otitis media means your child is in a lot of pain. Bacteria have infected the fluid in his ears. He is likely to experience symptoms including fever and ear pain that are caused by inflammation of the middle ear. He may be tugging on his ears a lot. Children ages 6 months to 24 months are most likely to experience acute otitis media, but preschoolers and early elementary school children can suffer from them, too.

Treatment for otitis media is typically a dose of antibiotics. Some pediatricians may watch and wait out the infection for several days before prescribing any medication.

Otitis media can also lead to a **ruptured eardrum** (rip or tear in the eardrum) caused by pressure created by the fluid in the middle ear. The eardrum usually heals within three months and typically no treatment is recommended. Another possible consequence of otitis media is **cholesteatoma**, which is a growth of skin cells in the middle ear. Cholesteatoma can grow large enough to cause damage to the ossicles. Treatment for this condition is surgery.

▶ OTITIS MEDIA WITH EFFUSION

Otitis media with effusion refers to when there is a buildup of fluid in the middle ear that could become infected. When the fluid is thick and white, ENTs call the condition **glue ear. All this fluid in the middle ear does not allow the ossicles to move properly, causing a conductive hearing loss** that can range in severity from slight (meaning your child will have trouble hearing soft sounds like a whisper) to mild (she'll have trouble hearing soft speech) or moderate (she will have trouble hearing conversational speech). If the fluid in your child's ear is not infected, she will not receive antibiotics, and it can often take two to three months for fluid to drain completely and your child's hearing to return to normal.

▶ RECURRENT ACUTE OTITIS MEDIA

Recurrent acute otitis media refers to multiple, separate episodes of ear infections over the course of several months. Some kids are more prone to ear infections than others, depending on the shape of their ears, noses, and sinuses. Dr. Michelle witnessed this condition in her own household: her first daughter, Annabel, suffered from several ear infections before she was three. Her younger daughter, Charlotte, had no ear infections before the age of three. Although the two girls look very similar, they have slight differences in their anatomy—not visible to the rest of us—that resulted in different symptoms from a common cold.

An ENT may recommend **pressure equalization (PE) tubes**, also called **grommets**, if a child has experienced multiple episodes of ear infections as well as allergy or sinus issues. These tubes are placed in the eardrum surgically and allow the pressure in the middle ear to equalize. This is a pretty simple surgery that typically occurs in an outpatient setting at a clinic or hospital. Sometimes, the tubes fall out and your doctor has to put in a new set if your child is continuing to suffer ear infections.

A relatively new device, called an **EarPopper,** can be used to open the Eustachian tube to equalize pressure so the fluid can drain.

▶ ACUTE EXTERNAL OTITIS

Acute external otitis, or **swimmer's ear**, refers to an infection in the outer ear canal caused when bacteria grows in water that remains in the ear canal after swimming. The good news about swimmer's ear is that it can usually be treated with eardrops.

PARENTING TIP

LOTS OF KIDS get ear infections; they are one of the most common reasons for visits to the pediatrician. But Dr. Michelle has a few ideas about how to prevent them:

- **Don't let your baby fall asleep drinking a bottle.** The liquid can pool in her mouth, allowing it to enter the Eustachian tube.
- **If you can, nurse your baby.** Babies who are breast-fed are less likely to experience ear infections.
- **Don't smoke.** Babies who are around cigarette smoke are more likely to have ear infections.

SENSORINEURAL HEARING LOSS

Sensorineural hearing loss is the result of damage to the inner ear hair cells or nerves that carry information to our brain. Unfortunately, sensorineural hearing loss is permanent. Once a person's hair cells are damaged, there is no medication or surgery to repair them. However, there are some treatment options to help children hear better. Hearing aids amplify or make sound louder. Another treatment used for children with severe to profound hearing loss is a **cochlear implant**, a device surgically implanted in one's cochlea, in the inner ear, that acts like hair cells by sending electrical impulses to the auditory nerve when sound enters the ear.

Children with severe sensorineural hearing loss usually learn to communicate verbally, but may also communicate in other ways, such as through American Sign Language.

Genetic Conditions

Babies born with sensorineural hearing loss typically have underlying genetic conditions. These babies may be deaf or may suffer from partial hearing loss. Remember that the vast majority of babies born deaf have hearing parents. If your baby was born with sensorineural hearing loss, you or your partner may have had an uncle or a distant cousin who was deaf. Or you may have been surprised: that's because parents may be carriers of a recessive gene that causes hearing loss and will not necessarily anticipate a hearing problem in their baby. **Waardenburg syndrome**, a group of conditions passed down through families that may involve deafness as well as pale skin, hair, and eye color, has a dominant genetic pattern and can also cause sensorineural hearing loss at birth.

Infections and Ototoxic Drugs

Illnesses accompanied by very high fever, often stemming from bacterial meningitis, mumps, and measles, can cause sensorineural hearing loss. Also, medication used to treat these illnesses can damage hearing. These **ototoxic drugs,** which can cause damage to the hair cells of the inner ear, are often antibiotics that end in the suffix "-mycin," such as neomycin or streptomycin.

PARENTING TIP

THERE ARE AVAILABLE vaccines for many of the illnesses that can cause high fever that in turn may lead to hearing loss. We strongly suggest having your child vaccinated.

NOISE-INDUCED HEARING LOSS

Have you ever felt that you can't hear well after going to a concert or a loud bar? There's a medical term for that: Excessive exposure to loud noise can cause **noise-induced hearing loss**. If you visited that noisy environment only occasionally, then your hearing loss is simply temporary and can return to normal. But **if loud noise is present for long periods of time on a regular basis, then the hearing loss can be permanent.** Children and babies are exposed to many noisy environments, and that level of noise is typically not limited by any regulatory body. There are lots of noisy environments that your child may experience, but one often overlooked is the neonatal intensive care unit (NICU). The medication, machines, and equipment needed to help sick babies can potentially damage your baby's hearing. Babies who spend long periods of time in the NICU may not respond to loud noises and sounds the way other infants do.

PARENTING TIP

KEEP THE VOLUME down on your TV, radio, smartphone, and tablets. If you have to raise your voice to speak over the TV or music, even slightly, then it's too loud.

Helping a Child with Sensorineural Hearing Loss

If your baby or child is diagnosed with sensorineural hearing loss, there are a few options to help them hear you. Today, there are many types of hearing aids that are quite powerful in making sound louder so that it can be heard. Hearing aids require no surgery, so they can be used with very small babies. Hearing aids can be very expensive—often totaling thousands of dollars—and they are not always covered by insurance. Different types of hearing aids abound; if you are in the process of selecting a hearing aid, consider the device's battery life. Hearing aid batteries often need to be changed several times a week. Hearing aids that use rechargeable batteries may be a good choice for you.

Another treatment that is used with children who have significant hearing loss is a cochlear implant. Cochlear implants require surgical implantation of wires in the inner ear as well as an external device, and in the United States they can be implanted as early as 12 months after birth. Cochlear implants wipe out existing hair cells, so any residual hearing would be lost when the device is implanted, representing a risk for this treatment option especially for children who have some hearing. Cochlear implant technology has come a long way since it was first introduced. Today, most children with significant hearing loss who receive a cochlear implant are very successful oral communicators.

Parents of children with hearing aids or cochlear implants may also want their child to use a **frequency modulation** or **FM device** in their home and the school the child attends. This small piece of equipment, worn by an adult, transmits your voice directly to the child's hearing aid, like a personal radio.

No matter what treatment you, and your audiologist, and ENT decide on, the earlier the treatment, the better. One thing to keep in mind is that hearing aids and cochlear implants are imperfect tools. If you wear glasses, your vision will be restored when you put them on; the same is not true for hearing aids and cochlear implants. They help people hear better, but they don't restore hearing completely. Kids who use hearing aids and cochlear implants need to learn how to use them. Over time, they gradually improve their ability to discern different sounds and frequencies.

While kids with hearing aids and cochlear implants may learn to communicate verbally, they often, but not always, experience speech and language delays.

TESTING, TESTING, TESTING

Kids today are lucky. Audiologists have many different methods to test hearing in babies, toddlers, and kids. The development and popular spread of hearing tests over the past several decades is great news for kids (and their parents!) because more and earlier testing methods have led to earlier detection of hearing loss. Until relatively recently, a child's hearing loss was usually detected when he was in preschool or early elementary school, well after the child showed delays in language, speech, social, or academic development. Research supports that the earlier a hearing loss is detected and treated, the better the child's speech and language development and academic achievement later on.

Here's the lay of the land on the different testing options.

NEWBORNS

Today, nearly all states require newborn hearing tests. All states have Early Hearing Detection and Intervention programs that give extra support for newborns who suffer hearing loss.

Newborn hearing testing typically takes place in the hospital where your child was born. If you are planning a home birth or your birth center does not provide hearing testing, your baby's hearing can be tested in a pediatrician's or audiologist's office. **Some kids are considered especially at-risk for hearing loss, including babies who are placed in the NICU.**

Your baby can't raise his hand when he hears a beep, so audiologists use a special way to test his hearing. This test uses a probe to send a sound into your baby's ear. Audiologists measure the response of a baby's hair cells, also called **otoacoustic emissions**. A healthy ear will send a sound back out, like an echo. In an ear with hearing loss, no sound will come back. Babies need to be still and quiet to pass this test, so the audiologist at the hospital may whisk away your baby when she is asleep in order to test her. She may even be tested while she is feeding, as long as she is quiet.

Another way to test hearing in infants, or those who are hard to test—such as children with autism—is by measuring a child's **auditory brainstem response (ABR)**. For this test, sensors placed on your baby's head measure the auditory nerve and brain's response to sound.

TODDLERS

A toddler's hearing is not routinely checked by an audiologist or pediatrician. That's where you come in. If you, another caregiver, or a medical professional suspects your child may have hearing loss—possibly because he seems to have a speech and language delay—then it's time to visit the audiologist.

Toddlers are not good at sitting still but they can let us know that they can hear different noises through their behavior. Audiologists often use a testing method called **visual reinforcement audiometry**. For this test, which can be used with children as young as 6 months and up to 24 months, your toddler is taught to look at a toy after he hears sounds from a nearby speaker. Your child will hear a sound and see a fun-looking toy light up or move; he will then realize that hearing the sounds prompts the toy to light up, and he'll keep searching for the sound to come—usually a beep or an instruction from the audiologist. Audiologists can measure how well the child can hear the sounds by observing the child's behavior.

PRESCHOOLERS

Hearing in children three to five years old can be tested using **play audiometry**, in which the child listens for a sound or beep and then drops a block in a bucket, or adds a ring onto a ring stacker, when the beep is made.

At this age hearing screening is often performed as a part of your child's annual well visit to the pediatrician's office. **If your child has not received a screening by the time he's off to kindergarten, it's time to talk to your pediatrician.** You want to make sure your child can hear the teacher properly.

SCHOOL-AGE CHILDREN

Some elementary schools perform hearing tests for children, but this is hardly the gold standard, because some groups (like the U.S. Task Force on Preventive Services) don't recommend routine hearing tests for school-age kids while other groups (like the American Academy of Pediatrics) do. **If your child isn't getting his hearing tested in school, you should ask your pediatrician or regular medical professional about routine testing.**

DR. MICHELLE'S TAKEAWAY

YOU KNOW YOUR child best . . . If at any point you suspect she or he is experiencing a hearing loss or not acting as you would expect, schedule a hearing screening with an audiologist. A healthy baby's hearing is typically tested once soon after birth—and then not again for at least another three years. That's a long time.

RED FLAGS
What to Look Out For and When

Your child may be displaying signs that she's not hearing properly. Here are some specific things to look out for.

○ **If your child is experiencing a speech or language delay.** Fortunately for you, we wrote two chapters on speech and language development in this book. Please consult Chapters 2 and 3 for the age milestones for speech and language development. If your child isn't meeting them, his hearing should be evaluated so call up an ENT or audiologist and ask for a hearing test.

○ **If your baby is not responding to loud noises.** Newborns sleep a lot, but when your baby is awake and alert, she should respond to loud noises like a siren or pots and pans clanging. Her response should include looking toward the sound, jerking her body, or even crying. If she's not regularly responding to loud noises, then it may be time to get her hearing checked.

○ **If your baby is pulling on his ears or if your older child is complaining of ear pain or jaw pain.** He may have an ear infection. Go visit your pediatrician.

○ **If your child is suddenly asking *What?* or *What did you say*?** This is a very common sign that your child may be experiencing temporary hearing loss due to an ear infection. As we mentioned previously, ear infections can cause a conductive hearing loss. It's time to go to the pediatrician *and* get your child's hearing checked.

○ **If your child is older than a year and is not responding to his name.** It's time to visit the audiologist. Babies who are 12 months old—and even younger—respond to their name when it is called. If your baby is not looking toward you or does not pause from her playtime when you call her name, you must discuss this with your pediatrician. Not responding to one's name by 12 months can be a warning sign for hearing loss or for a developmental delay.

COMMON QUESTIONS,
EXPERT ANSWERS

Fortunately, Dr. Michelle is married to an audiologist, Dr. Mike. Over the years, they have answered hundreds of questions from parents about children's hearing. Here are some common questions and their answers.

QUESTION: *My daughter failed her newborn hearing test, and now we have to get a follow-up. Should I be worried?*

ANSWER: Don't freak out just yet. It is not uncommon for your baby to fail the newborn hearing test in the hospital. When your baby was born, she had fluid and mucus all over her body, including in her ears. It can take a few days for the ears to become clear, which can interfere with passing a hearing test. Babies born premature or diagnosed with a known genetic condition, like Down syndrome, are more likely to be born with hearing loss. Be sure to have a follow-up appointment scheduled within one or two weeks.

QUESTION: *I'm sick of hearing* Frozen *for the sixteenth time, so I have made my daughter listen to the movie with headphones. Will this affect her hearing?*

ANSWER: It can if the volume on the headphones is too loud. Repeated exposure to loud noises can cause noise-induced hearing loss, which is permanent. You child's ears are smaller and usually more sensitive than your ears, so sounds that may be comfortable to you could be too loud for her. Consider setting the volume for your child at a level that sounds soft to you.

QUESTION: *Will my child grow out of ear infections?*

ANSWER: Yes. Ear infections occur most frequently in children under three years. Young children's Eustachian tubes are more horizontal, so fluid can easily get trapped and infected when your child has a cold. Although older children and even adults can experience ear infections, they are much less common after age 8.

QUESTION: *My child seems to tune me out when he is playing. Can he hear me?*

ANSWER: Probably. When young children play, they can be very intense and seem to ignore you when they are concentrating on puzzles, art projects, or Legos—that's normal. **If your child doesn't respond to you when she is looking at you or is not engrossed in an activity, it's time to see your pediatrician and/or an audiologist.**

QUESTION: *My toddler doesn't seem to hear me well and I see a lot of wax in his ear. Can I use a Q-tip to get it out?*

ANSWER: Absolutely not; you need professional help. Earwax, also called **cerumen**, is important for protecting the ears: It traps and collects foreign objects such as dirt, debris, and bugs. Wax sits along your ear canal; at the end of the ear canal lies your eardrum. However, a large accumulation of earwax can create a blockage, causing temporary hearing loss. We know; you see all that gross wax in your child's ear and want to get it out. But don't reach for a Q-tip to get the wax out of your child's ear: You are likely to push the wax in further, and because kids have shorter ear canals than adults, it is possible to rupture your child's eardrum if you push the Q-tip too far. A wet washcloth is the best way to remove earwax that is visible. An audiologist or ENT can use a special medical instrument to extract the wax that's really lodged in there. Don't try it at home!

DR. MIKE'S CLASSROOM TIPS

BEFORE YOUR CHILD trots off to school, you might want to think about the noise she will be exposed to in the classroom. Classrooms are noisy. Other students are talking (or, likely, screaming), air conditioners or fans hum and whirl, and hallway conversations compete with the teacher's voice. There is often background noise from outside sources such as lawn mowers, construction work, and children playing at recess. These sounds can bounce off hard surfaces like walls, chairs, and desks and interfere with what the teacher is saying.

Noisy classrooms can negatively affect auditory comprehension, reading and spelling, concentration, and overall academic achievement in all children. Children with particular learning difficulties—such as kids who have hearing loss, attention difficulties, speech and language delays, and those whose first language is not English (or the language of instruction)—are particularly affected by noisy learning environments.

Dr. Mike suggests reducing the noise in classrooms:

- Install carpet, rugs, or foam tiles on the floor or part of the floor.
- Hang curtains or blinds on the window.
- Hang absorbent material on the walls, such as cork board or fabric (e.g., flags or student artwork, especially art that contains different textures).
- Place split tennis balls or felt pads under chair legs.

Work with your child's teacher to reduce background noise. All children in the classroom will benefit, and so will the teacher. She will not have to talk louder to talk over the noise.

A PARENT'S PERSPECTIVE

Marlowe's Story

Marlowe was a strong and healthy infant, but she failed the newborn hearing test in the New York City hospital where she was born. The hospital's staff audiologist and nurses assured Marlowe's parents that she probably just had fluid in her ear, advising them to follow up with her pediatrician. Her parents took her to the pediatrician for more hearing tests several times over the next few months, but she never passed them. Nonetheless, Marlowe's parents were certain she could hear; no one in any of Marlowe's extended family had hearing loss. "We were in denial," Marlowe's dad recalls.

However, after two auditory brainstem response tests, it was clear: Marlowe had severe hearing loss in one ear and moderate-to-severe loss in another. Genetic tests didn't turn up a clear reason. Her hearing loss was simply a mystery.

The family decided to try hearing aids for Marlowe when she was 4 months old. The result: She was transformed. "I was not prepared for the stark difference," her dad says. "She was finally turning her head to our voices. She was a different kid." When the family dog stirred in a nearby room, Marlowe would look up; she could finally hear his footsteps. Life with hearing aids wasn't always easy, of course: Marlowe would try to take them off (her dad used tape to keep them on), and her parents worried that even with the hearing aids, she would not develop the proper verbal skills to communicate in a hearing world.

Soon thereafter, Marlowe began receiving speech therapy several times a week at home, and when she turned 2 she attended a nursery school for kids with hearing impairment. "When Marlowe went in, she wouldn't speak, and when she left she wouldn't shut up," her father says. "They turned on that part of her brain." Marlowe now attends a mainstream classroom at a local elementary school, where she continues to receive group speech therapy services. She is reading on grade level, socializes with her friends, and talks like a champ.

SOME SIMPLE THINGS TO DO AT HOME

Parents can do a little bit to help protect their child from hearing loss. As we've said before, we live in a very noisy world—one that's getting even noisier with the prevalence of high-tech gadgets in our lives. So here are Dr. Mike and Dr. Michelle's tips to keep things quiet on the home front:

- Put duct tape over the speakers of your child's noise-producing toys to reduce loudness.
- Keep the TV, radio, or computer at a volume level low enough to avoid having to raise your voice to speak over it.
- Buy earplugs or protective headphones (they look like ear muffs) for your child. We know—you might not see a lot of kids wearing them. But once upon a time, seat belts and bike helmets weren't trendy either. We think hearing should be the next child safety concern. Consider earplugs or protective headphones in noisy environments like at parades, concerts, wedding receptions, or on noisy bus or train rides.
- Download a free—or really cheap—app to measure decibel levels in the environment around you.

RESOURCES

There is a wealth of information about kids' hearing available online, from sites that focus on hearing impairments and disorders to sites that help you find ways to protect your child's hearing. Here are some favorites according to Dr. Michelle and Dr. Mike:

○ The Food and Drug Administration, which regulates hearing aids as medical devices, publishes a guide about different hearing aid options and how to choose the best one for your child's needs: *http://www.fda.gov/medicaldevices/products andmedicalprocedures/homehealthandconsumer/consumer products/hearingaids/default.htm.*

○ The American Speech-Language-Hearing Association (ASHA) has a lot of information about hearing development and disorders: *http://www.asha.org/public/.*

○ The American Academy of Audiology, a professional group for audiologists, hosts a website that helps parents learn more about hearing loss and find specific information on corrective devices, such as hearing aids. It also contains a link to finding an audiologist: *http://www.howsyourhearing.org/index.html.*

○ The National Institutes of Health (NIH) is another source of information about hearing loss in children: *https://www.nlm.nih.gov/medlineplus/hearingproblemsinchildren.html.*

○ The Sight and Hearing Association publishes a yearly report in November of the noisiest toys and provides the loudness levels of these toys: *http://www.sightandhearing.org.*

2

SPEECH

The Road to Mastering Sounds

B ABIES ARE BORN to make sounds. In the beginning, that mostly means crying. But gradually, your baby will start to utter sounds that sound, well, human. Eventually, she'll put these sounds together to make words. At first, those words may be ones that only you can decipher. Later, her words will start to sound like the speech of a preschooler. Eventually, as your child grows, she'll start to pronounce her words just like you do.

There are two main components to your child's communication. One is **speech**, the other is **language**. In this chapter, we'll differentiate between the two and then focus on speech—what it is, how it develops, what you may be likely to notice about your child's speech development as it progresses, the potential red flags your child may exhibit, and when and how you should address any of these problems.

WHAT'S SPEECH, ANYWAY?

You know all about speech and language because you use them every day, but you may not know the definition of each term. The two are often used interchangeably, but they refer to different things.

Speech describes the physical and motor movements needed to produce sounds and syllables and words and sentences. Think of it this way. Speech involves air flowing up from your lungs through your voice box or **larynx**, and then moving your jaw, tongue, and lips to create sounds. **Language is what the sounds mean or represent.**

To illustrate these two concepts, let's take a sentence that Henry, a three-year-old boy, tells his mom: *I wike ice cweam.*

Makes perfect sense, right? Henry built a sentence that followed the rules for ordering words correctly in English, included sounds we use in English all the time, and expressed a particular meaning that would be understandable to all English speakers. Without even knowing it, Henry used language to express his thoughts—he likes ice cream!

But the way that Henry uttered some speech sounds—his pronunciation—was different from how an adult would do it. He made a *w* sound instead of an *l* sound in the word *like*. And he made a *w* sound instead of an *r* sound in the word *cream*. If an adult said those same words in the same way, it wouldn't sound quite right. But Henry's speech sounds like a typical three-year-old child.

One important characteristic of speech development is that the way children make certain sounds varies considerably with age. What we might consider a mistake for an older child would be perfectly appropriate for a young learner. Henry's speech would actually be quite precocious for a two-year-old, whereas for a five-year-old it might be cause for concern. But for a three-year-old, he's pronouncing the words just as he should be.

HOW DOES SPEECH DEVELOPMENT HAPPEN?

One rule of growing up very much applies to speech development—it's gradual. In the pages that follow, you'll see that process of speech and sound development.

Babies practice their speech skills long before they say real words. Their speech then continues to develop and progress for many years after they utter those first words and start to form rudimentary sentences.

You might think of your child's first year as a big rehearsal for the second year, when he will actually take sounds and string them together into recognizable words. The second year, of course, is a rehearsal for the third, when his speech will start to become comprehensible to all sorts of people, from caregivers to peers to strangers on the street.

It takes several years for children to figure out how to correctly say all the sounds we use in our speech every day, whether we're speaking in English, French, Mandarin, or Swahili. But this doesn't keep children from trying, which is why you get all sorts of cute and silly word pronunciations from toddlers. Among our favorites, taken from our own kids: *ganks* instead of *thanks, wove* instead of *love*, and *pida* instead of *pizza*.

Typically, children master all the speech sounds of their primary language by the time they are in the second grade, around age 7 or 8. As with everything having to do with childhood development, even typically developing children frequently experience bumps along that very long and windy road to big-kid land. We'll explain what this road looks like for a typically developing child, and you can figure out if that's a road your kid is on. If it isn't, we'll provide some tips for you to get her to a good place.

MOVE THAT MOUTH, BABY!

For babies and toddlers, learning to talk has a lot to do with motor development of the mouth—just as learning to walk has a lot to do with motor development of the arms, legs, and trunk.

Fine-tuning the motor skills of the mouth takes time. When babies learn to walk, they usually achieve a lot of milestones in between (rolling over, sitting up, scooting, crawling, and cruising). When babies learn to talk, they have a long journey before their jaw, mouth, tongue, and lip muscles are fine-tuned enough to make many of the sounds that we use to put together to form words. This period of speech development is characterized by mastery of some sounds as well as the gradual ability to say others.

In newborns, the jaw, tongue, and lip muscles are immature. While they are perfect for their age and size, babies aren't able to make adult-quality speech. They haven't developed the crucial fine-motor and coordination skills yet to make the sounds that adults or big kids make effortlessly every day. And let's be honest—they haven't had a lot of practice making the human sounds we make, either.

Speech requires your baby to coordinate three systems in her tiny body.

○ **First, there is the physical action that babies (and all humans) make with their mouth, jaw, tongue, and lips to form words.** Speech and language specialists describe this complicated ballet of the jaw, tongue, lips, and the soft palate as **articulation.**

○ **Second, babies also need to practice phonation,** or vocal cord vibration. This allows them to make certain speech sounds, like the z sound, as well as vowels.

○ **Third, babies use their respiratory system when producing speech.** We need to take in a breath, and we talk while exhaling. When they are just born, babies are concentrating on using their lungs just to stay alive. But eventually, they need to figure out how to coordinate their respiration with their articulation and phonation so they can breathe and talk all at once. It's easy for us. Not so easy for little tykes.

··

FROM RESEARCH TO REAL LIFE

··

BABIES ARE CONSIDERED to be **universal speech perceivers**, meaning they can hear the difference between speech sounds that are in the language they are exposed to (such as English) as well in languages they have never heard before. Researchers such as Peter Jusczyk and Patricia Kuhl have found that babies lose the ability to perceive differences in speech sounds that are not in the language they are exposed to by the time they have reached their first birthday.

This means that babies can learn the speech system of any language starting at birth. But as they get older, they become more sensitive to the speech sounds they hear every day, they pay attention to those sounds, and they block out sounds that are not important.

LET'S LOOK AT DEVELOPMENTAL MILESTONES IN SPEECH DEVELOPMENT

Babies all around the world develop their speech in the same way. Whether your baby is born hearing Spanish, English, or Russian, her speech sound milestones (again, different from her language milestones) are going to be the same.

Scientific researchers such as John Locke and Carol Stoel Gammon have observed what babies say when they make speech sounds, and they have found that all babies, no matter what language they are exposed to, follow a similar path of speech sound development. All babies, in their first year of life, will produce similar sounds when they babble. This is because they say sounds that are easiest to produce—usually the *b*, *d*, and *m* sounds.

While it's true that babies the world over follow a similar path in their development of speech milestones, we want to emphasize that the keyword is similar: No two paths are identical. Typically developing babies will begin to say certain sounds—with and without meaning—within a similar time frame.

PARENTING TIP

AS LONG AS your child is hitting her speech sound milestones at some point during the appropriate age range, her speech development is considered to be progressing typically. It doesn't matter if she is hitting the milestones at the early end or the late end of that range.

Now, we'll take you through the journey of those first few years of life—from the first cries of your baby to the smooth-talking words of a kindergartner.

FROM 0 TO 2 MONTHS

Babies produce **reflexive**, or **involuntary**, **sounds** such as cries (sorry, Mom and Dad—expect a lot of them), grunts, coughs, and burps. They also produce other sounds and noises during feeding called **vegetative sounds**. These are your baby's way of telling you what his needs are. His vocalization may be telling you, *I'm hungry, I'm tired,* or *Yum, that tastes good.*

Your baby will spend a lot of time crying in his first two months. But all of this crying is not for nothing: These cries, although reflexive in nature, do have communicative functions. For example, a baby's hunger cry is different from his tired cry, which is different from his discomfort cry.

And as if they weren't loud enough during their waking hours, it is not unusual for babies to be really noisy in their sleep. Those grunts may come out a lot at night, so if you feel like you are sharing a room with a baby piglet, that's okay—it simply means your little one is practicing the movements needed to make more sounds.

All these sounds that your baby makes are related to the size and shape of his or her mouth. When children are first born, their tongues fill up the majority of their mouths, leaving little room to move it to make speech sounds. Your baby also has **sucking pads**, or fatty deposits in her cheeks, which helps her to extract liquid when drinking. So the kinds of sounds that babies make when they are very young do not resemble adult speech sounds—or even the sounds that an older baby makes.

DR. MICHELLE'S TAKEAWAY:

EXPECT CRYING AND other sounds as your baby learns how to tell you what she needs and wants.

FROM 2 TO 4 MONTHS

Your baby should begin to make his first **cooing sounds**. These are vowel-like sounds such as *oohs* and *aahs*. Babies this age also make lots of gurgling sounds. Because they are still unable to sit upright by themselves, your baby will spend a lot of time on his back, and his tongue will fall to the back of his mouth. So expect a lot of sounds like *grrr* and other **guttural sounds**—or sounds made in the back of your throat.

PARENTING TIP

IT'S TIME TO start your job as communication encourager-in-chief. As a parent or caregiver, you want your child to learn that speech and language are an interactive game. They learn from you. So try to get your baby to coo as much as possible. Cooing has a way of making those long days packed with feedings and diaper changes seem a little less monotonous. Plus, it's great for your child to learn to take **vocal turns**—figuring out how to look into the eyes of Mom or Dad or a caregiver and experimenting with as many sounds as possible.

As the cooing picks up, your baby will eventually begin to laugh. A baby's first laugh is often like a pitched cry of glee, rather than an outright giggle. Do your best to elicit it from your child—in other words, try to engage your baby by doing the kind of ridiculous acts that might get a good laugh out of him. (True fact: Whenever she wanted her kids to laugh, Carlyn sang the Beatles song "Yellow Submarine." Worked every time.)

There is some more good news at this age: **At around 12 weeks, the frequency of a baby's crying usually decreases.** This tends to make Moms and Dads very happy. It also means your baby should have more time to practice his cooing skills.

DR. MICHELLE'S TAKEAWAY

EXPECT cooing and laughter.

FROM 4 TO 6 MONTHS

Your baby will start to discover her voice. These can be fun times. You'll hear loud cooing, soft cooing, medium cooing, and all sorts of extremes in loudness and pitch. You'll hear squeals and yelps and high-pitched and low-pitched sounds. When you drop something on the floor, you may hear your baby react with a yelp or a giggle. You may have an amateur opera singer in the house, testing her scales throughout the day.

You will also hear **vowel sounds** (such as *a* and *eh*) as well as some **consonant sounds** (such as *d* and *b*). The consonant-like sounds are likely to be sounds made in the back of your baby's mouth.

DR. MICHELLE'S TAKEAWAY

EXPECT ENTHUSIASTIC COOING, yelps, and laughter.

FROM 6 TO 9 MONTHS

Your baby will learn a new, big, important skill: **babbling**. Your baby has begun to string consonant and vowel sounds together.

There are two kinds of babbling your baby will perfect:

1. **Reduplicated babbling** is what you'll hear when she says the same consonant-vowel pattern over and over, such as *babababa* or *mamamama*.
2. **Variegated babbling** is what you hear when she varies the consonant-vowel pattern, such as *badaba* or *wadaba*.

Your baby's physical development helps her to begin babbling. At around 6 months, most babies begin to sit upright, unsupported, and now have more room in their mouths compared to when they were newborns. Your baby's tongue no longer fills up her entire mouth and her sucking pads have dissolved. Now, she has more motor control over her jaw, tongue, and lips, which allows her to make some new, adult-like speech sounds.

All babies, no matter what language they are exposed to, will produce similar sounds when they babble. Remember, they say sounds that are easiest to physically produce. These sounds include the consonants *m*, *b*, *d*, and *n* and short vowels *e*, *a*, *i*, *o*, and *u*.

DR. MICHELLE'S TAKEAWAY

EXPECT BABBLING WITH at least two different consonant sounds.

Some babies may start babbling a bit earlier than 6 months and others a bit later, but if your baby is not babbling by 8 months, it may be time to think about what's going on. Is she really perfecting her motor skills? Is her hearing okay—does she respond to loud noises? Does she have an ear infection? Check in with your pediatrician if you aren't hearing any babbling by this time; meanwhile, keep engaging with your baby. **Some Simple Things to Do** are provided later in this chapter, so consult that section.

FROM RESEARCH TO REAL LIFE

THERE IS A lot of research that suggests so-called **prelinguistic** sounds, or the sounds babies make before they really start talking, are very important for later language development. Some noteworthy scientific studies show that the more sounds babies make when they are infants, the better the language skills they have as children. Here are some things scientists know about prelinguistic sounds:

- The more sounds a baby makes at 3 months, the bigger her vocabulary is likely to be when she is two and a half years old.
- The more mothers and fathers respond to infant vocalizations, the more infants vocalize.

What should you do at home? **Encourage babbling and vocalizations. Respond to your baby's sounds, even if they don't seem to be meaningful.** This will inspire him to vocalize again.

FROM 10 TO 12 MONTHS

Babies shift into a new phase. They start to speak in what speech and language specialists call **jargon**. Remember the Swedish Chef character on *The Muppets*? In nonscientific terms, babies sound like the Swedish Chef, putting together consonant-vowel combinations that have all the intonations of your speech. But these sounds don't actually mean anything—yet. Your baby will sound like she is talking to you, telling you what she wants or sharing a long story. (Carlyn was always pretty sure her sons were sharing their opinions on world politics.)

Practicing sound combinations is how babies get ready to say real words. The more they practice, the better they get. While they are in this jargon stage, they will continue to produce babble, as they had before, but they are now experimenting with putting sounds into more complex combinations.

DR. MICHELLE'S TAKEAWAY

EXPECT JARGON, or sounds strung together that sound like real words.

We know—you're busy. So, in Figure 2-1, we have presented some of the key milestones for your baby's first year. In the rightmost column you can check off when your child makes these sounds and the age when you first notice them.

Figure 2-1. Prelinguistic vocalizations.

AGE	TYPE OF VOCALIZATION	AGE OBSERVED
Birth to 2 months	✓ Cries (hunger cry, tired cry) ✓ Reflexive sounds (sounds during feeding indicating pleasure, burping)	
2 to 4 months	✓ Cooing (*oohs* and *aahs*) ✓ Laughter (loud and soft, belly laughs and little giggles)	
4 to 6 months	✓ Vocal play (variation in loudness and pitch, squeals and throaty sounds)	
6 months +	✓ Babbling (strings of consonant—vowel sounds such as *dadadada* and *badawa*)	
10 months +	✓ Jargon (strings of sounds that have adult-like intonation, as if your baby is having a conversation with you, in his or her own baby language)	

WELCOME TO ONE

Congratulations! Your baby has celebrated her first birthday. Guess what? This means that she is starting to enter a whole new territory as a talker. It means she is moving to the land of words.

Around age one, babies start to say their first words. Notice that we say "around" age one. **Do not worry if your baby's first birthday comes and goes and she doesn't have a word yet.** We'll get to the topic of typical milestones for first words in Chapter 3, but as with everything having to do with childhood development, we are talking about a range here.

Speech development is very much related to language development. Research shows that the more sounds babies produce in babble, the more words they will have, and the more practice babies and toddlers have saying speech sounds in their words, the easier it will be for them to say new words.

When babies start to say their first words, the sounds are similar to the sounds they have been practicing as they babbled. For example, if a baby frequently says *bababa* in his babble, it's likely that his first words will contain a *ba* sound, and he might be partial to words like *baba* for *bottle* or *ba* for *ball*. In contrast, a baby who said *ma* a lot in his babble might start saying words like *mama* for *mommy* or *mo* for *more*.

Over the next six months, babies gradually add more and more words to their vocabularies, and the sounds in these words are likely to be the ones they practiced the most when they were babbling and jargoning up a storm. This means you will probably hear a lot of words that begin with *ba*, *ma*, and *da*.

As your one-year-old continues to practice speech, you may notice that she may prefer words with the same sound. Dr. Michelle's first daughter had many first words with the *h* sound: *hat, hot, hi, hop,* and *Heather* (her favorite aunt). Dr. Michelle's second daughter was quite partial to the *b* sound, and her first words included *book, ball, bus,* and *bye-bye*. However, you may also hear your child form a new sound or word and then not use it for a while. That's common and totally okay.

EXPECT REAL WORDS that contain sounds your baby practiced when she was babbling.

WHAT DID HE SAY?

HAVE A HARD time understanding your toddler? You're not alone. The term to describe how well you can understand someone is called **intelligibility**. As your child grows, his intelligibility improves.

FROM 18 TO 24 MONTHS

Toddlers become better and better at communicating. They use real words, but also rely on gestures (such as pointing) and vocalizations (such as saying *eh-eh-eh!*) to get their needs met.

Most children experience a **vocabulary spurt** during this time—when they add new words to their repertoire each week.

This vocabulary spurt is matched by a **speech sound spurt**. To keep up with all those new vocabulary words, kids add more speech sounds to their repertoire. Children this age will continue to use the speech sounds they practiced during babble and jargon as well as their first words, but you might also start to hear new sounds such as *f, w,* and *h*. You may also hear your child using short, simple words that contain these sounds, such as *hat* or *fish* and maybe some variation on *water*.

Even though kids this age are starting to be able to say new sounds, they still can't say all the sounds and syllables that adults use every day in their words. But, somewhere deep down, they must know this, and so they start to come up with some pretty clever ways to basically substitute their own sounds and patterns for what they might hear from their parents, caregivers, older siblings, or other kids at daycare—but can't yet say themselves. Speech and language specialists refer to these efforts as **phonological processes**.

Here are some common things toddlers do at this age as they use their new ability to make sounds into words but still confront limitations in what they can say:

○ **They repeat the first syllable of a two-syllable word,** so *bottle* becomes *ba-ba*, *water* becomes *wa-wa*, and *raisin* becomes *rai-rai*. Specialists refer to this as **reduplication**.

○ **They lop off the final consonant of a word,** so *cup* becomes *cu*, *car* becomes *ca*, *ball* becomes *ba*, and *night-night* becomes *nai-nai*. Specialists call this **final consonant deletion**.

○ **They delete a syllable that isn't stressed,** so *banana* becomes *nana* or *Cheerio* becomes *i-o*. Specialists call this **syllable deletion**.

○ **They lop off a consonant from a blend of consonants,** so *blue* becomes *bu*, *truck* becomes *tuck*, or *school* becomes *cool*. Specialists call this **cluster reduction**.

Of course, your child's limits in speaking can sometimes cause frustration for your child—and maybe for you. One reason children this age can sometimes seem like they are on an emotional roller-coaster is because they so badly want to communicate all their needs—but can't.

WHAT DID SHE SAY?

DON'T BE SURPRISED if it takes a little while to figure out what your 18- to 24-month-old child is saying. He's just getting the hang of learning to speak. At this age, it is likely that his primary caregivers are the only people who can understand him. And it's perfectly okay if you have no idea what your child is saying quite a bit of the time.

TWO-YEAR-OLDS

By now, you've surely observed that your toddler is entering her so-called **terrible twos**, a stage of development when a child's behavior is particularly challenging. While this may make for some interesting times behavior-wise, it simply means that she is changing day by day, picking up new skills and testing her independence. One of the things she is working on is her speech skills; chances are your toddler is rapidly improving her ability with speech sounds. During this year, toddlers add more and more sounds to their repertoire, and their speech is likely to become much more recognizable both to parents and others. You might not find yourself acting as an interpreter when Grandma comes over.

Here are some things that kids between ages 2 and 3 will pick up:

○ **They will start to say the end of words,** so the 18-month-old who said *ba* will likely say *ball*, and *ni-ni* will likely be *night-night* by the time he's around age 2.
○ **They will start to say all the syllables in words,** so a child who might have said *nana* as an 18-month-old can now start to say *banana*.
○ **They will add more and more sounds to their repertoires** and are likely to especially focus on perfecting the *p*, *b*, *m*, *n*, *w*, and *h* sounds.

Even as they are picking up new sounds, typically developing two-year-olds still struggle with certain sounds, and they do plenty of things to simplify their speech to make life easier for themselves and avoid saying the sounds that are tricky, just as they did when they were a bit younger. Here are some things typical two-year-olds do to adapt their speech:

○ **They will make the first sounds in a long word more accurate than the later sounds.** So *water* might be *waa-er*. Note that that's a big improvement over *wa-wa*, which a child might have said when she was 18 months.

○ **They may simplify sounds that are hard to say by saying a sound that is easier.** For example, the *s*, *sh*, and *th* sounds are more difficult than the *t* sound, so you may hear *tun* instead of *sun*, *to* instead of *shoe*, and *tank you* instead of *thank you*. Specialists refer to this as **stopping**.

○ **They will still have trouble with consonant blends**, just as they did when they were younger. So your child may continue to lop off a consonant from a blend of consonants, so *blue* becomes *bu*. Or she may just substitute a sound that she finds easier to say, so *blue* becomes *bwu*.

As two-year-olds mature, they'll gradually come to rely on these adaptive mechanisms less frequently and their words will sound clearer.

WHAT DID HE SAY?

AS YOUR TWO-YEAR-OLD matures, you'll be able to understand more and more of what he says. You can expect someone who is not with your child every day to understand about 50 percent of what your child says. Remember, her **intelligibility**—her ability to be understood by others—will improve as she ages.

If most people can't understand about half of what your child says by age 3, you might want to consider checking in with a speech language therapist.

DR. MICHELLE'S TAKEAWAY

SOMETIME AFTER TWO, your child's speech will become clearer. Expect your child to begin to say whole words like a big kid does!

THREE- AND FOUR-YEAR-OLDS

By the time your child turns age 3, and then moves on up to age 4, she has graduated from being a toddler to being a preschooler. Think about how her speech reflects her new position in life; she's now starting to talk more and more like a big kid and can communicate her ideas with words that are understood by other kids as well as teachers and other parents. **Preschoolers can generally speak in full sentences and are continually practicing and improving their speech sounds.**

Here are some things kids ages 3 and 4 should be able to do:

○ **They should be able to say all vowel sounds.**
○ **They should begin to master other sounds, such as k, g, f, and v.**
○ **They should begin to master the ability to say new sounds, such as y and l.**

Despite all their accomplishments, preschoolers will have trouble with some common sounds. You can expect them to:

○ **Have trouble with the r and l sounds.** These are really tricky sounds for three- and four-year-olds to say. Of course, some kids may master them early, but don't be surprised if your four-year-old still has a hard time with these sounds.
○ **Get tripped up with certain sounds in the middle of words.** It can be hard for kids to coordinate their articulators (remember, the jaw, tongue, and lips) from one sound to another,

which makes sounds in the middle of words or at the ends of words difficult. A child who has just gotten the hang of the *l* sound may be able to say *lamp* or *lunch*, but not *balloon*.

○ **Have trouble with the *j* sound.** Words like *juice* and *jump* might be hard to say.

○ **Have trouble with consonant blends.** Remember how your two-year-old couldn't say *blue*? While some kids may have mastered consonant blends by age 4, if your child isn't there yet it's perfectly okay.

○ **Have trouble with *sh*, *th*, and *ch* sounds.** Words like *shark* or *shoe*, *thumb* or *thank*, or *cheese* or *chicken* may all be tricky for your kid. No worries!

WHAT DID SHE SAY?

BY THE TIME your child is age 3, you should understand most of what she says; by the time she's age 4, you should understand pretty much everything she says.

Your child should become more and more intelligible to people other than parents and caregivers who see them every day. Someone like a friend or neighbor who is not caring for your three-year-old every day should be able to understand 75 percent of what she says. By the time your child is age 4, a friend or neighbor should be able to understand 90 percent of what she says. If your child is not there, it's time to consult with a speech language therapist.

DR. MICHELLE'S TAKEAWAY

YOUR CHILD'S SPEECH should become quite clear. Don't worry if he or she is still having trouble with a few sounds.

SCHOOL-AGE CHILDREN

By the time your child is a big kid and has entered kindergarten, she should be able to say most of her speech sounds. She may have trouble with certain sounds, like *r* and *s*, but **for the most part, children this age have mastered all the speech sounds of the English language.** Children who are ages 5, 6, and 7 may also have trouble with multisyllabic words, like *spaghetti* or *kindergarten*, and may also be using some phonological processes (those systematic ways to simplify speech) in order to say these difficult sound sequences. For example, consonant blends are hard to say, so many times children insert a vowel between two consonants, saying things like *balue* instead of *blue*, or *gareen* instead of *green*.

At this age, it is important that children can say all or most of their speech sounds accurately, because they will soon be learning their letters and letter sounds, one step in the process of learning how to read. Figure 2-2 shows the mastery of all the consonant sounds in English and the age at which most typically developing children have mastered the sound.

Figure 2-2. Speech sound mastery.

AGE (years)	SOUND	EXAMPLE
2	P	pie
	B	boy
	M	more
	N	no
	H	hot
2 ½	W	winter

(Box Continues)

AGE (years)	SOUND	EXAMPLE
3	T	**t**oy
	D	**d**og
	K	**k**ite
	G	**g**o
	F	**f**ish
4	Y	**y**es
5	V	**v**an
	L	**l**ight
	J	**j**udge
	Ch	**ch**eese
	Sh	**sh**oe
6	S	**s**un
	Z	**z**oo
	R	**r**abbit
	S blends	**sn**ow
	R blends	**gr**een
	L blends	**bl**ue
6½	Th	**th**ank

SOURCE: Adapted from Janet Barker Fudula, *Arizona Articulation Proficiency Scale, Third Edition* (Los Angeles, CA: Western Psychological Services)

DR. MICHELLE'S TAKEAWAY

AT ANY AGE, if you think your child is not at the same place her peers are, or if you have concerns about your child's speech development, Dr. Michelle suggests you consult with a speech and language professional. This is *especially* important for kids who are at or approaching school-age. If a child is having difficulty with many speech sounds, she may have difficulty learning the letters and speech sounds needed for literacy development because **phonics**, or letter-sound correspondence, is an essential building block of learning to read. See Chapter 5 for a more in-depth discussion.

 RED FLAGS
What to Look Out For and When

Not all kids master their speech milestones right on time. But the good news is that with a little help, you may be able to catch some of these issues early.

Dr. Michelle has identified the top eight red flags that she's noticed over her years as a speech language therapist:

1. If your baby is not babbling by 8 months: You want to be hearing those *babas, mamas,* or *dadas.* Remember, these sounds don't have to mean anything—in fact, they often don't—and your baby need only be saying one vowel-consonant sound combination to meet this milestone. But if he isn't babbling yet at this age, consult your pediatrician or healthcare provider.

2. If your baby is not producing jargon by 12 months: Your child should have perfected the art of talking like an adult—but with words that have no meaning. It's okay if your baby doesn't say any real words yet, but you should expect him to be stringing speech sounds together.

3. If your baby is not saying two to three words that contain a couple of different sounds by 16 months: There is an age range at which children begin to say words, but we expect them to say a handful of words by 16 months. These words should contain two to three different speech sounds. If your baby consistently says something along the lines of *mama*, *dada*, *up*, and *baba*, she's all set. If your child is not saying any words by 16 months, check in with your pediatrician.

4. If you can't understand at least half of what your two-year-old is saying: Sometimes it seems like your two-year-old is saying something with perfect authority, but you have no idea what it means. That's fine—it can be hard to decipher all of your child's words. But if you can't understand about half of what she says, you should monitor her; if you still can't understand about half of what she says at two and a half, you might consider getting a speech evaluation. See Chapter 8 for more details.

5. If you can't understand most of what your three-year-old is saying: Then it's really time to look carefully at his speech development.

6. If your preschooler is not saying her *k* and *g* sounds by age 3½: These are difficult sounds for kids to make. Both the *k* and *g* sounds are made in the back of your mouth and are harder to say than those sounds made in the front of your mouth, like *t* or *d*. However, by the time a child is age 3 ½, she should be saying those back-of-the-mouth sounds.

7. If your child doesn't improve her speech patterns every six months, starting at one year of age: By age 4, she should have acquired most of her speech sounds.

8. If your school-age child is not saying *s, r,* and *l* sounds or sound blends (like *bl, st, tr*) by age 6: These sounds are difficult to say and are late to be mastered, but by the time your child has completed kindergarten, he should be able to say them. Why? Being able to accurately say speech sounds is important for literacy development. Also, the longer a child says speech sounds a certain way, the harder it is to change. If your child has not developed these sounds on his own, it's a good idea to give him some extra help by consulting a licensed speech language therapist; we'll give more tips on how to find a great therapist in Chapter 8.

COMMON QUESTIONS,

EXPERT ANSWERS

Having been a speech language therapist to children for 15 years, Dr. Michelle has fielded a lot of questions from parents about their kids. One thing she has learned is that her answers to questions vary greatly depending on the child. Keep in mind that difficulty saying certain sounds may be developmentally normal for a kid one age, but for a child two years older it may signal an issue. Here are some of the most common questions Dr. Michelle gets from parents, and her tell-it-like-it-is answers.

QUESTION: *My child has had multiple ear infections. Will this affect her speech development?*

ANSWER: It may. Some ear infections can cause hearing loss, which in turn can affect speech development. See Chapter 1 for more information.

QUESTION: *Are there any mouth exercises that I can do with my child to help his speech development?*

ANSWER: No. Current research suggests that mouth exercises like moving your tongue back and forth, blowing, and practicing lip rounding (puckering) do *not* on their own improve the ability to make certain speech sounds. What improves the ability to say the right sounds is practice. In fact, that's what Dr. Michelle does in her daily work with kids—she gets them talking and talking.

QUESTION: *My five-year-old still struggles with the r sound. Is this normal?*

ANSWER: Absolutely. Kids master the r sound late because it is difficult to produce. It takes many years of practice to say this sound correctly. **About 90 percent of six-year-olds can say their r's correctly in all or most contexts.** If by the time your child is age 6 she isn't saying it correctly, it's time for her to get an evaluation from a speech language therapist. Consider it something to do over summer break or as fall approaches.

QUESTION: *My pediatrician recommended that my son get an evaluation from a speech language therapist—as well as from a feeding specialist. What's the connection?*

ANSWER: Some speech language professionals also specialize in feeding issues because children with motor delays may have problems eating properly as well as saying their speech sounds.

QUESTION: *Will extended use of a pacifier affect my child's speech?*

ANSWER: It is very possible, though not definitive, that extended pacifier use and/or thumb-sucking may influence the development and production of certain speech sounds because it affects dental arrangement. When a child has a pacifier in his mouth, he is not practicing his speech sounds and he's not honing his ability to say new words. Common sense tells us that kids who have things in their mouths much of the time are not getting a chance to practice their speech and language skills. The answer is to ditch the pacifier by age one, especially during the daytime.

QUESTION: *My child has problems with some speech sounds. Does this mean something is wrong with her dental arrangement?*

ANSWER: Sometimes yes and sometimes no. If your child has missing teeth, she may have trouble with certain speech sounds. Of course, every kid is going to lose her front teeth and may go through a period where certain sounds like s are a little off. That should go away once her permanent teeth grow in. If your child has teeth extracted when she is young—usually the result of poor dental care or a playground accident—her speech may be more permanently affected, depending on what teeth came out and when. Poor dental care can occasionally affect a child's speech development. Work on your child's dental care. Brush her teeth twice a day and don't let her fall asleep with a bottle or sippy cup in her mouth.

A PARENT'S PERSPECTIVE

Gabe's Story

Discovering and identifying a speech delay does not happen in a day. Take the story of the parents of Gabe, a three-year-old from Brooklyn, New York. As a baby, Gabe was lovely—happy, low-key, the kind of infant who cried only when he was hungry or tired. As Gabe got bigger, he seemed to do all the things other little kids did. Gabe's dad, who stayed home with Gabe while his mom worked, took him frequently to the playground, library, and play-dates, so he had plenty of chances to observe kids the same age. When Gabe was 18 months, his dad noticed that while other kids were saying a handful of words and even short sentences, Gabe was not saying much. Gabe's parents also had a hard time under-standing what he was saying. Gabe would stand by the fridge in the kitchen and point, saying *eeeeee*, which his parents finally understood to mean *milk*.

At his 18-month checkup, Gabe's pediatrician said he seemed fine. But at Gabe's two-year appointment, his parents pressed the pediatrician and she recommended Gabe get a speech and lan-guage evaluation. The speech language therapist observed that Gabe had difficulty saying words that came easily to other two-year-olds, such as *mommy* and *ball*. Over the first few months working with a speech therapist, Gabe began to master sounds like *b, p, d, n, m*, and *h*. By age 3, he was starting to get closer to matching his peers.

"It took a year for him to say *fire truck*," said Gabe's dad. "It took a year for people to really understand him."

A tip from Gabe's parents: Especially with firstborn children, identifying a speech delay can take a long time. It's often some-thing you gradually notice about your kid.

A COMMON CONCERN: ARTICULATION DISORDER

It's important to look out for any of the red flags (discussed previ-ously) in your child. All children, of course, experience typical varia-tions in speech development, but some children may have particular difficulty mastering certain aspects of speech; when they have these difficulties beyond the point that most of their peers have mastered them, Dr. Michelle recommends dialing up a local speech language therapist.

The most common speech-related concern is an **articulation disorder**—a bit of a catchall term involving a difficulty with the motor processes needed to produce speech in a precise and efficient manner. (Chapter 7 discusses some less common speech-related disorders, including **apraxia** and **dysarthria**).

Children with an articulation disorder usually have trouble saying one or more speech sounds. Moreover, they consistently have trouble with those sounds—in words, in complete sentences, and even on their own. Specialists don't exactly know why some kids experience articulation disorders and others don't, but a systematic review of the scientific literature conducted by James Law, a professor of speech and language sciences in Australia, and his colleagues in 1999 estimated that as many as 25 percent of five- to seven-year-olds have an articulation disorder. So if your child has one, he's in good company!

Here are some common articulation disorders:

○ Children who **lisp**. They have trouble saying certain sounds such as *s*, *z*, or *sh*, and they distort those speech sounds each time they use them in words. When a child has a lisp, he is having trouble articulating the sound—he is not moving his articulators in the correct place or sequence in order to say the sound in the same way an adult does. Lisps are common for children under age 6, but if your child is older than that, Dr. Michelle recommends looking into speech therapy to remedy a lisp.

○ Children over age 7 who have trouble making the *r*, *l*, and *th* sounds. A child who does this consistently may make sound substitutions (saying *wed* instead of *red*) or sound deletions (saying *geen* instead of *green*).

○ Children over age 8 who have trouble saying consonant blends. Examples of errors in blends include sound deletions (*back* for *black*) or sound additions (*balack* for *black*).

Speech therapy, likely for a period of six months to several years, may be the solution to an articulation disorder, depending on the severity of the articulation issues. You will work with a speech language therapist to help your child practice saying speech sounds in words. Your child should practice the same things she learns with the speech therapist at home, too. Practice makes perfect.

SOME SIMPLE THINGS TO DO AT HOME

Every parent can do a little bit to help their child learn new speech sounds and improve the ones she might need to do some work on. This is, of course, as true for typically developing kids as it is for kids with diagnosed conditions. Children learn from their parents and their caregivers, which is why they need your help! So be sure to try Dr. Michelle's tips at home!

BABIES

Encourage vocalizations and babbling. The amount of babbling a baby makes has a direct correlation to the child's language skills later on. How do you encourage babbling?

- Respond by looking at your baby and talking back when she babbles or vocalizes. This will encourage her to babble again.
- Take turns to keep the conversation going. Respond after she vocalizes and wait for her to vocalize again. This helps her practice her language skills, which we will discuss more in Chapter 3. For example, after your baby says *babababa*, say, *Do you see the bottle? That's right, here's the bottle.*

TODDLERS AND PRESCHOOLERS

Once your child is older, he is talking in complete sentences, but he is not necessarily saying all his speech sounds correctly. That's okay; he still has plenty of time to perfect his sounds, and the more he practices, the better he is going to get. Remember that there are many speech sounds that he likely can't say. Don't worry—he will be making them before you know it. If there are some sounds that you think your child should be saying but is still having trouble with, try to get him to imitate your speech:

○ Have your child look at your mouth while you are speaking to her. Young children, starting at age 3, can look and learn where the articulators go.
○ Use play to practice speech sounds and incorporate it into your everyday routine.
  • If your child is having trouble with the k and g sounds, then practice saying those sounds when playing. For example, take a toy farm and say the words *cow, goat, goose,* and *cock-a-doodle-doo* (and stress the k and g sounds when you say the words). Then ask your child to repeat these words after you say them.
  • If your child is having trouble with the b or p sound, get him to say *beep beep beep* while playing with cars. Or practice *pop pop pop* and *bubble* while playing with bubbles.
  • You don't need a specific activity to work on speech sounds. Just practice saying speech sounds in words with your child while playing with her. It will be fun for you and your kiddo.

KINDERGARTEN TO FOURTH GRADE

If your school-age child is having difficulty with one or more speech sounds, try to practice these sounds at home. Older children may have more awareness of their speech, so you might be able to talk with them more openly about their articulators and where to place them for certain sounds.

Sometimes, a child simply needs these things brought to her

attention and then she can correctly say the sound in words. For example, saying "that color is not *wed*, it's *red*" may be enough for a child. At other times, children need much more practice in order to correctly say speech sounds, especially those that are tricky, like *r*, *s*, and *th* sounds.

○ **First, talk about how to say the speech sound,** explaining where your tongue and your lips go. For instance, if you are practicing the *th* sound, ask your child to look in the mirror and watch her tongue go between her upper and lower teeth.
○ **Say the sound first,** then have the child try.
○ **Practice listening** for that sound in words and sentences and talk about what letter or letters make that sound.
○ **Practice these sounds in your everyday routine.** If your child has a classmate named Ryan and you are practicing the *r* sound with your child, you may try saying his name in sentences and talking about what he did in school.

RESOURCES

We know—you really have more questions about your child, and you figure you can just handle it all by consulting Dr. Google. But it's hard to navigate all the information that is available on the internet. So we want to recommend information from websites that are up to date, accurate, and grounded in the latest science. Dr. Michelle has two favorite sites to recommend; both contain special pages on specific topics that are intended for parents:

○ The American Speech-Language-Hearing Association (ASHA), the primary professional organization of licensed and certified speech therapists, has resources for parents, caregivers, and professionals: *www.asha.org*.
  • One page has information about typical speech and lan-

guage development: *http://www.asha.org/public/speech/development/*.

- Another page has information about speech disorders: *http://www.asha.org/public/speech/disorders/speechsound disorders.htm.*

○ The National Institutes of Health (NIH), the federal agency that provides research on health matters, and a division of NIH called National Institute on Deafness and Other Communication Disorders (NIDCD) both have basic information about speech disorders:

- The NIDCD's home page provides some helpful information on the latest scientific research on speech and hearing disorders: *www.nidcd.nih.gov/Pages/default.aspx.*
- You will also find information about typical speech and language development on a specific page devoted to the topic at: *http://www.nidcd.nih.gov/health/voice/pages/speechandlanguage.aspx.*
- For information about speech disorders, see: *http://www.nlm.nih.gov/medlineplus/ency/article/001430.htm.*

3

LANGUAGE

The Key to Communication

S O MANY PARENTS love to talk about their child's first word. Was it *Mama*? *Dada*? *Banana*? *Dog* or *truck* or *cat*? We might think of a baby's first words as his gateway to language—as the first entry in a very long book of his life. But in many ways, that book begins at the start of infancy. Language development commences early in a baby's life, perhaps as early as in utero, and it extends well into the teenage years—and even beyond (even adults can learn new words!).

In this chapter, we will discuss how language development occurs, introduce you to various theories as to how we come to acquire language, help you identify important changes in your child's language development, point out potential red flags your child may exhibit, and talk through some of the most salient questions Dr. Michelle hears from parents about their children's words and how they use them.

WHAT'S LANGUAGE, ANYWAY?

Language is critically important to your everyday life, from your social interactions, to your ability to get your needs met, to your ability to express yourself. You use language every day. So do the people all around you. And chances are, **your baby is participating in the system of spoken language even if he's not officially talking yet**. That's because our ability to understand words long precedes our ability to say them.

You may not have ever thought about what language really means. Well, let's start big. Language is one way to *communicate*, to share information or ideas. There are other ways to communicate, too—among them using facial expressions, body language, and gestures such as pointing and waving—but in the context of this book's subject we'll limit our focus to language.

Scholars refer to language as a **symbolic system**, meaning that it is a system composed of symbols—such as spoken words, sounds, and sentences. These symbols are used to represent things like objects, events, people, and ideas. If you know the symbols—be they spoken words, sounds, or sentences—then you can use them to create meaning, to communicate. We use speech, or spoken sounds, to turn these symbols into words.

Languages are constantly changing. New words are added and used all the time (think *Google*) while other words become less prevalent (think of all those unfamiliar words in a Shakespearean text). Languages do not have to be spoken, though; some are considered **manual languages**, or **signed languages**, and they use hand gestures as symbols. These manual languages, such as American Sign Language, have all the components of a spoken language.

Each language, whether it's a spoken language like English or Mandarin, or a manual one like American Sign Language, has its own set of rules. If you know the rules, you can make sense of things you have never heard of or said before. We know, for example, that in English the following sentence isn't correct: *The hugged mommy baby the*. But if we arrange the words in a different order—*The mommy hugged the baby*—then the sentence makes perfect sense. Once your child truly understands the symbols and rules of a language, the possibility for creating new ideas and expressions are endless.

Regardless of whether you're speaking English, ancient Hebrew, or

Japanese, linguists have divided language into five main components: semantics, phonology, morphology, syntax, and pragmatics. These component parts are what your child will be perfecting over time as he begins his journey into spoken language—even if he's not aware of it!

- ○ **Semantics** refers to the meaning of a word in a given language. Take the word *dog*. It means an animal that can be kept as a pet, is furry, has a tail that wags, and says woof.
- ○ **Phonology** describes the rules of combining speech sounds to create words. For the word *dog*, you combine *d* + *o* + *g*.
- ○ **Morphology** delineates the rules of combining parts of speech—what people in English commonly refer to as **grammar forms**—to create words. So, if you wanted to make *dog* possessive, you would add the *'s* making it *dog's*. The word *dog's* has two **morphemes,** or two meaningful units.
- ○ **Syntax** concerns the rules of combining words and phrases into sentences. The sentence *My dog's name is Spot* follows the rules of English syntax.
- ○ **Pragmatics** pertains to the rules and conventions of the social use of language. These include practices such as maintaining eye contact, taking turns, staying on topic, and beginning and ending conversations. All are important skills that children learn over time, some more easily than others.

HOW DOES LANGUAGE DEVELOPMENT HAPPEN?

It's pretty amazing that kids learn first languages with no formal instruction. Most kids learn the primary language that they are exposed to over the course of several years, in a completely effortless manner. Sure, they don't master all of the rules of language at once—they learn some of those component parts at different times—and they often make what adults consider to be mistakes along the way, but this is all part of the learning process. Language requires cognitive processing that develops over time. Most of us don't remember learning our first language; it just happened. (We'll talk more about learning second languages in Chapter 6.)

Typically, children master the majority of linguistic rules by the time they are in the second grade, around age 7 or 8. Even after that age, they continue to acquire more vocabulary words, and as they get older, they are typically able to understand and use more abstract and figurative language.

Learning a language is a journey that takes years; in many ways, it is never complete. It is one of the most joyous, exciting, and sometimes hilarious parts of childhood development. But all those high points can sometimes be accompanied by frustrations and low points, too. In this chapter, we'll explain how a typically developing child acquires language to help you determine if your child is doing the same. Mastering spoken language is a thrill in itself. But it is also an entry point to the next milestone. **When young kids master spoken language, they are well positioned to embark on another big undertaking in their lives: learning to read.** We want to help your child learn to use her words so that she can express herself, make friends, talk to peers and grown-ups, and eventually use all those words to develop her literacy skills when she's a big kid. At the end of this chapter, Dr. Michelle provides some tips for you to encourage your child to develop and enrich her language—a lifelong gift, no doubt.

LANGUAGE THEORY 101

A range of specialists study language and how it develops in individuals and in society at large. Among them are **linguists**, scholars who study the parts and structures of languages. A whole host of specialists have made key contributions to the field of linguistics, including philosophers, psychologists, neuroscientists, and speech-language pathologists, who are also known as speech language therapists.

The process of learning a language is called **language acquisition**, and research is constantly evolving to understand how exactly children acquire language. While scholars have been studying this topic for centuries (Plato was interested in how we acquire language, too), linguists in the previous century developed a number of theories to explain the process of language acquisition that are widely accepted today:

- **Behaviorism**, a theory pioneered by American psychologist B. F. Skinner, suggests that language is a learned behavior, similar to other skills such as playing the piano. In this model, children hear language and begin to associate it with a particular item or action. Parents or caregivers shape children's linguistic behavior.
- **The linguistic model**, championed by American linguist Noam Chomsky, suggests that humans are all born with the ability to learn language—that it's a universal and uniquely human characteristic. One merely needs to expose a child to a language and he will figure out the important rules for that language.
- **The cognitive approach**, originated by Swiss developmental psychologist Jean Piaget, suggests that language is a general cognitive skill, and that once a cognitive skill is acquired, certain language rules can be acquired. For instance, once a baby understands the concepts of cause and effect, she can learn to achieve desired effects with vocalization, such as crying and saying words such as *up*.
- **The social interaction, or sociocultural, approach**, developed by Russian psychologist Lev Vygotsky, suggests that language is dependent on social interaction—that babies want to engage in social interactions and language is a mature way for them to interact. As children interact with others, their language, as well as other important cognitive processes, develops.

There is evidence to support and refute all of these models of language acquisition. And research into language acquisition continues to evolve: In recent years, linguists, computer scientists, and statisticians have joined forces to examine language acquisition in children, often by analyzing vast troves of electronic data documenting when children learned certain words.

FROM RESEARCH TO REAL LIFE

MORE IS BETTER when it comes to talking to your children. In the 1990s, two researchers, Betty Hart and Todd Risley, recorded everything that was said over the course of two and a half years to 42 young children who were just beginning to use words. The researchers found that children whose families were talkative became talkative as well, and that children who were exposed to less language were less talkative. An important correlation was found between the family's income and the amount of time they spent talking to their kids. Families with high incomes talked to their kids more than families with low incomes.

Throughout this project, whose findings were published in an article called "The Early Catastrophe" in the journal *American Educator* in 2003, Hart and Risley discovered what they called the "30 Million Word Gap"—children from poor families hear 30 million fewer words by the time they are three years old as compared to their peers whose families are financially advantaged. This research has generated public health projects in cities and states across the country, encouraging parents to talk to their children. **The bottom line: Talk to and engage with your child. They are carefully listening to and absorbing the language around them.**

──── **DR. MICHELLE'S TAKEAWAY** ────

IT IS VERY LIKELY that language is the result of many factors—cognitive, social, behavioral, and environmental.

LET'S LOOK AT DEVELOPMENTAL MILESTONES IN LANGUAGE DEVELOPMENT

What words children know and what words they can say is the subject of great fascination to linguistic researchers. Today, researchers use many techniques to understand what children know about language, from recordings taken in children's homes to studies involving eye tracking, electrophysiology, and play-based experiments.

Researchers study the development of both **receptive language**, what kids comprehend, and **expressive language**, what kids say. We know that receptive language generally precedes expressive language—a baby typically understands the word *mommy* before she can say "mommy." In the sections that follow, Dr. Michelle describes the major receptive and expressive language milestones that you should observe from your child. These milestones generally fall in four categories: vocabulary, grammar, syntax, and pragmatics, with some change-ups, depending on the age.

We know how busy you are, so Dr. Michelle has also created a handy chart with key language milestones (see Figure 3-1). Use it to check off when your child acquires more words and skills.

Figure 3-1. Language milestones.

AGE	RECEPTIVE LANGUAGE MILESTONES	EXPRESSIVE LANGUAGE MILESTONES
0-6 Months	✓ Quiets when hearing familiar voices ✓ Pays attention to music	✓ Smiles in response to people ✓ Vocalizes pleasure and sadness
6-12 months	✓ Listens when spoken to ✓ Responds to own name ✓ Shows excitement in response to caregiver approaching ✓ Links words to objects and actions	✓ Babbles with consonants and vowels ✓ Produces jargon ✓ Imitates different speech sounds ✓ Uses gestures to communicate, such as pointing, clapping, and waving
12-18 months	✓ Attends to object names ✓ Understands many words that are used every day ✓ Can point to some body parts	✓ Babble and jargon continue ✓ First words appear (between 9 and 15 months) ✓ Vocabulary increases by one or two words per week
18-24 months	✓ Follows simple and familiar one-step directions ✓ Points to familiar toys, people, household items, and pictures	✓ Vocabulary spurt occurs—period of rapid word acquisition (one to two words/day) ✓ Simple two-word utterances ✓ Basic grammar forms include plurals (*cats*) and present progressive (*running*)
2 years	✓ Points to body parts, clothing ✓ Follows one-, two-, and even three-step familiar directions ✓ Listens to stories and points to pictures when asked	✓ Utters one, two, and three words ✓ Has a vocabulary of 300+ words ✓ Talks about events in the past and future ✓ Uses words to ask questions, comment, get attention, and protest

AGE	RECEPTIVE LANGUAGE MILESTONES	EXPRESSIVE LANGUAGE MILESTONES
3 years	✓ Understands words for colors, shapes, and sizes ✓ Knows the sequence of events of simple stories and procedures	✓ Has a vocabulary of 1,000+ words ✓ Speaks in sentences containing three, four, or five words ✓ Maintains the topic of conversation ✓ Uses adult grammar forms more frequently (frequent mistakes common)
4 years	✓ Understands most words that adults say ✓ Comprehends simple *who*, *what*, and *where* questions	✓ Strings two to three sentences together ✓ Forms sentences containing four to five words ✓ Begins to master grammar forms that were difficult at age 3 ✓ Can rhyme words
5–6 years	✓ Begins to understand figurative language ✓ Demonstrates metalinguistic skills ✓ Understands grammar and syntax rules	✓ Masters many grammar forms ✓ Takes the listener's perspective when speaking ✓ Acquires new vocabulary and words that have more adult-like definitions; new words may reflect school knowledge

Remember that all children develop at their own speed. **The milestones Dr. Michelle discusses are met by the majority of typically developing children in a specific order**. Kids don't always follow the same road as their peers—and yet they get to the end just fine. It's possible that your child is not doing the exact same things as her peers at the exact same time, but she'll likely end up in the same place before long. Sometimes, though, kids need extra help in getting there. We'll provide you with some tips to help you find out if your child might need assistance. You'll find even more advice on getting help in Chapter 8.

FROM 0 TO 12 MONTHS

Linguists and speech therapists refer to the first year of your baby's life as the **prelinguistic period**—the time when she is acquiring the building blocks for spoken language, although she can't yet speak. In her first year, your baby is listening to all aspects of language and learning the rules of the language being used around her. She is soaking in some of those key pragmatic language rules, such as maintaining eye contact when speaking to another person and learning **vocal turn taking**, the process of letting speakers take turns and listening and waiting while others are speaking.

PARENTING TIP

DON'T BE AFRAID to use **infant-directed speech,** sometimes referred to as **motherese**—the singsong way that we talk to babies and young children, in a slow, simplified manner with big changes in intonation. We help babies find the important words in our speech by elongating them, bringing the baby's attention to them. It helps to focus your baby's attention to objects—by pointing, gesturing, or giving the object to the baby—and to talk about events that are happening. **This language helps your baby link words to actions and objects.**

Babies understand words long before they can say them. They can also identify important words that they hear frequently. By the time your baby is one year old, and possibly well before, he should respond to his own name. That is a key sign that he has good hearing and is demonstrating basic receptive language skills. Babies' reactions can show us they understand the words and phrases we use: If your baby hears that mommy's coming, he may get excited about your arrival.

Before he turns one, your baby is practicing the skills he needs to say words. Remember all those *bababas* and *mamamas* we referred to in Chapter 2? When babies babble, caregivers generally respond in a way that encourages more babbling. There is a positive relationship between the amount of babble and early vocabulary development. Kids who babbled more as infants have been shown to have larger vocabularies later on, compared with babies who babbled less. Babies who babble more say more words, and the more caregivers respond to baby's babble, the more babies babble.

Even though your baby is not yet saying words, he will be able to communicate with you more and more as he approaches his first birthday. Starting when your baby is around 10 months old, you should observe him using gestures such as pointing, clapping, and raising his hands to indicate *up*. These gestures are a major entry point to spoken language. They show that your baby can express herself to get her needs met.

DR. MICHELLE'S TAKEAWAY

BEFORE YOUR BABY says his first word, he is getting ready to talk by listening to language and practicing sounds.

WELCOME TO ONE

Well, you made it to your baby's first birthday, and chances are you are starting to listen for his first word. **There is a large range in which typically developing babies begin to say real words.** Some babies say their first word as early as 9 months, and some wait a little later, until 14 or 15 months. Remember, your baby is learning lots of new skills during this time—like walking—so if she is focusing on one of those skills, she may not get to her first words until after she masters another milestone.

Vocabulary

First words may be magical, but sometimes it can be hard to figure out just what the magic is. Your one-year-old is still mostly talking in jargon. So you will have to pick out the words from the jargon. Your baby has likely been saying *mama*, *dada*, and *baba* in her babble since she was around 6 months old, but these sounds were just vocal play and not real words. A **word** is considered to be a form that is similar in sound to (but not exactly the same as) the adult form of the word, that is said on a consistent basis, and is symbolic—meaning that it's used to refer to an object, action, or event. If your child says *dada* while playing with toys, it doesn't count as a word. If she points to her father when he enters the room and says *dada*, then you've got a word. Other utterances that count as words at this age (and are often frequently said as early words) include *uh-oh*, *night-night*, *vroom*, and animal sounds such as *moo*, *woof*, and *meow*. Saying someone's name—like an older sibling or the name of a pet—counts too.

At first, vocabulary growth is slow. **Once babies begin to say real words, they typically add about one to two new words every week.** First words are usually high-frequency words that represent important people, things, or events, such as *mama*, *dada*, *book*, *up*, or *bye-bye*. Toddlers tend to add nouns to their vocabulary because they are easy to represent and are tangible. Caregivers tend to bring attention to objects and label the names of objects for babies, as in, *Look—pause— here's a CAR!* This allows the child to focus on the word and encourages him to incorporate it into his own vocabulary. Nouns usually make up at least 50 percent of early vocabularies, but your child may also add some action words like *do*, *go*, and *eat*; adjectives like *hot*, *cold*, and *dirty*; and greetings or expressions like *hi* and *bye-bye*. *No* is also a popular first word. Your child might have one key pronoun in his vocabulary: *mine*.

Remember from Chapter 2 that your child's speech is also still developing, and she won't be saying these words as clearly as an adult will. But you should notice that the sounds your child has been practicing in her babble will appear in her first words. Although your toddler has started to use real words, she will also still babble, use jargon, yell, and cry.

Early words may have multiple meanings. If a 14-month-old says *doggie*, he may mean *there is a doggie, I want the doggie*, or *the doggie ate the food*. With limited vocabularies to express all these ideas, babies will change their inflection to communicate different meanings.

You may also notice that your baby calls all animals doggie. He has learned that *doggie* means a furry animal with four legs, so he'll call other creatures with these characteristics *doggie*. This is called an **overextension**. Once kids have practiced paying attention to different attributes of animals, they will begin to correctly label *cat, cow, horse*, and *pig*, too.

FROM RESEARCH TO REAL LIFE

CHILD LANGUAGE RESEARCHERS, including the American developmental psychologist Katherine Nelson, have identified different types of word learners. **Referential learners** systematically learn single words (mostly nouns) and add these words to their vocabularies one at a time. When they say these words, they can say them fairly accurately. Referential word learners seem to be careful and systematic. **Gestalt learners** learn nouns and phrases as whole chunks. Their early words may include *thank you, excuse me, I love you*, or *give me*. Although adults view these as phrases, the child learns these sound combinations as single words. A gestalt learner may not say the sounds in their words or phrases as clearly as referential learners. Carlyn and Dr. Michelle both have two kids—one gestalt learner and one referential learner each.

Understanding Language

Your child should definitely be responding to her name by now. When you point out key objects, she should look at them. Her receptive language skills are ahead of her spoken language skills: At 12 months, babies may say three words, but understand about 50 words.

DR. MICHELLE'S TAKEAWAY

EXPECT YOUR BABY to say his first words around his first birthday. He will slowly add more and more words to his vocabulary.

FROM 18 MONTHS TO 24 MONTHS

While you may have heard true words coming from your child's mouth only sporadically before 18 months, after this point she will likely cross a threshold into a period of more language expression.

Vocabulary

Sometime between 18 and 24 months your toddler will have a **word spurt**, or a rapid acquisition of vocabulary words. This word spurt occurs approximately six months after babies say their first words, when their vocabularies contain around 50 words (remember, animal sounds, names, and expressions like *ouch* still count). While your child was once acquiring one or two words a week, he's now gaining one or two new words a day. Most of your toddler's vocabulary will consist of **content words**—nouns, verbs, adjectives, and adverbs. She may be repeating everything you say and wanting to know the label for everything in sight.

Grammar and Sentences

Around the time that your toddler is experiencing a word spurt, he will begin to form rudimentary first sentences. Kids this age create simple two-word sentences like *More milk*, *Bye mama*, *My book*, and

Eat cookie. In this stage, toddlers will continue to use one-word utterances, babbling, and jargon, but by the time your child is two, she should be using *real* words more often than babbling, jargon, or gesturing. The short sentences that toddlers say are not grammatically correct. As they get closer to their second birthday, you should notice toddlers beginning to use basic grammar forms. Kids typically master the present progressive first—for a grammar refresher, those are verbs ending in *-ing*, like *running, sleeping, eating.*

Understanding Language

Toddlers still comprehend more words than they can say. They can follow simple one-step directions that are part of their daily routines, but may not understand all of the words in a sentence, especially if they are not said in the context of their regular routine. Your child should also be able to point to familiar toys, people, and household items when asked.

DR. MICHELLE'S TAKEAWAY

EXPECT YOUR TODDLER'S language to explode. He will learn many new words and combine his words into short sentences.

TWO-YEAR-OLDS

Over the course of this year, most typically developing two-year-olds show tremendous language growth. They begin their second year saying simple two- to three-word sentences and end the year saying longer sentences, using grammar and employing language to express their own thoughts or ideas. Along with language growth, expect a tremendous amount of cognitive, behavioral, emotional, and physical growth.

Vocabulary

Two-year-olds will continue to add more and more words to their vocabularies. **By the time they are age 3, they can say more than 1,000 words!** They say so many words that parents cannot keep track of what they can say. Nouns will continue to be the most common words in their vocabularies, but they will now start to expand their word list with more verbs; pronouns (*he*, *she*, *we*, and, of course, *me*); articles (such as *a* and *the*); quantifiers (words such as *one*, *two*, or *a lot*); adjectives (such as *little* or *big*); and auxiliary or helping verbs (such as *to be*).

Your child's vocabulary will continue to reflect her everyday life. Most of the time, a child will be talking about the here and now but may begin to talk about events in the past or future. Kids this age have a pretty interesting—or, shall we say, not entirely accurate—understanding of time, and their language reflects that. They may use *when I was a baby* to denote anything in the past or *tomorrow* to indicate anything that will happen in the future.

Pragmatic Language

Two-year-olds use their expanding vocabularies to express a variety of communication functions—to ask for things, to protest, to comment, and to regulate the topic of conversation. Toddlers also will start to use politeness markers such as *please* and *thank you*—usually, ahem, when reminded by an adult.

Once your child turns two or two and a half, you might start to have some early dinner table conversation with her. At this age a child can typically take two to three turns when discussing a particular topic. Don't expect the discussion to focus on world politics; your child's preferred topics will be related to present or past meaningful events in her life, like going to the beach or zoo. Your two-year-old is fairly self-centered, so you may find that the best conversation you have with her is about her.

Language can be frustrating, too. Children this age can encounter the limits of their language and have trouble broadcasting their wants, needs, or opinions. Two-year-olds are working on developing strategies for handling **communication breakdowns**, when an initial message is not effective, and their strategy is often to repeat the same words multiple times or simply to say them louder, even if they are not understood. Of course, don't be surprised if that strategy fails and what ensues is a good old-fashioned temper tantrum.

Grammar and Sentences

Two-year-olds can put together two, three, and four words into sentences. Once your child approaches his third birthday, he may even be using longer sentences. But these sentences are not always grammatically correct. Children often delete parts of speech or words like articles, and their sentences may not have subject-verb agreement. A typically developing two-and-a-half-year-old may say *I go sleep now*, or *I want milk, please*, or *They is running*. Kids this age frequently stumble on what pronouns to use, and that's okay.

Kids this age do something called **over-regularization** of past tense and plurals. They take the common practice of, say, adding an *-ed* to make a verb past tense or an *-s* to make a plural and apply it universally; so they'll say, *I runned* or *I ated the cakeses*. **When kids make these mistakes, they show us that they are learning the rules of language.**

Two-year-olds also begin to form rudimentary questions by inserting question words—usually *what*—into simple sentences, such as *What doggie doing?*

Kids this age are able to use the correct syntactic rules for the language they are exposed to. In English, for example, kids will follow correct word order, but they will leave out small words along the way. It would be unusual for a child to use the incorrect word order, saying something along the lines of *Sleep now I go, or Milk please want I.*

Here are some key grammar forms to listen for when your toddler turns two:

○ **Combines two words** using the conjunction "and" (*cereal and milk*)
○ **Forms regular plurals** (*books, crackers, cars, dogs*)
○ **Says "in"** (*cereal in bowl*)
○ **Says "on"** (*hat on head*)

Here are some key grammar forms to listen for when your toddler turns 2½:

○ **Uses possessives** (*Mommy's, doggie's*)
○ **Uses the irregular past tense** (*I ate Goldfish*)
○ **Uses the regular past tense** (*Mommy kicked the ball*)
○ **Uses articles** (*the book, a ball*)
○ **Uses the third-person regular verb form** (*Daddy hits the ball*)

It's perfectly okay if your child starts to use some of these grammar forms when she is age 3. Keep in mind that grammar forms take quite some time to master, and many kids will at first make many mistakes.

Understanding Language

Your two-year-old will continue to understand more than he can communicate or say. And watch what you say, because he can understand a lot! He should show you that he knows body parts like his belly or nose by pointing to them when asked. Following directions is an important way your child can show you that he understands you. Your child should be able to follow familiar directions, even those with multiple parts—for example, *Pick up the blocks and put them in the box*. Have we said this loud and clear yet? Keep talking to your two-year-old!

DR. MICHELLE'S TAKEAWAY

YOUR CHILD WILL begin to master rudimentary grammar forms and put together short sentences. She can use language to express some, but not all, of her intentions.

PARENTING TIP

THE BEST WAY to teach your child great vocabulary, grammar, and syntax is through modeling. That's when you show, often through repetition, the correct way that language is used. So when your child says *Doggie runned park,* you can repeat back to her, *Oh yes, the doggie ran to the park!* It might get old to you, but it will not get old to your child. This is how she learns.

THREE-YEAR-OLDS

You may notice that your three-year-old doesn't seem to stop talking. She is learning to become your conversational partner. Many three-year-olds seem to talk, and talk, and talk.

Vocabulary

Three-year-olds can say about 1,000 words—and understand many more. They acquire more and more words each day. Your child may say a new word—like *exhausted* or *terrible*—and you or your caregiver will ask, *Where did he learn that?* A three-year-old's vocabulary should contain all types of words, including nouns, verbs, adjectives, adverbs, and articles. Your child should speak in sentences containing three, four, or even five words. She should be able to correctly say the names of friends or relatives.

Your three-year-old should be learning and beginning to use

relational terms—words that compare objects or ideas to each other, including big or small, more or less, same or different. She should also learn descriptive terms, such as colors and attributes such as hot and cold.

Pragmatic Language

Three-year-olds learn to become conversational partners. They should be able to maintain the topic at hand (such as Sarah's birthday party) for two or three turns. Children this age can also begin to chain together familiar events, like a visit to Grandma's house, but the events may not be in the correct sequence.

Kids this age continue to learn most of their language skills and interact most through language with their parents and daily caregivers. It's perfectly fine if your child is not comfortable speaking conversationally with everyone around her. Just as kids this age are learning how to play collaboratively, they are still learning the social conventions of language.

Three-year-olds also pick up a new skill called **communication repair**—that is, they begin to vary their language to make the listener understand them. If your child says, "Mommy, I want it," and you didn't understand what he was referring to, he may vary his language, saying, "No, Mommy, I want that cookie."

Your child's personality may begin to really come out through his language. Your three-year-old may use language that is bossy, shy, silly, imaginative, cheerful, or sad.

Grammar and Sentences

Three-year-olds continue to practice adult grammar forms using plurals, possessives, and the present progressive. At this age, a child should be speaking about herself in the first person, saying *I eat birthday cake.* Other pronouns continue to be hard, though, and some kids do not master them until they are older (e.g., age five or six).

Your three-year-old should be using basic subject-verb-object sentence structures, such as *The boy is kicking the ball*. A two-year-old who wanted to express this same idea may say *boy kick ball* or *boy kicking ball*, but a three-year-old can likely include the article "the" in a sentence and the helping verb "is."

An older child will begin to master the art of asking a question as adults do, not just by using intonation, but by using the correct order of question words such as *What is . . . ? Who is . . . ? Can I?* and, of course, *Why?*

Understanding Language

Three-year-olds are able to follow simple directions with spatial, size, and color concepts: *Get the big ball, put the block under the table, and put on your red shoes*. When talking to your child, keep it literal: Three-year-olds do not understand figurative language such as *your eyes are bigger than your stomach*. They can understand the sequence of events of simple stories and procedures, like making a snowman, so it's a good idea to step up some of your conversational chatter with your child; use a varied vocabulary and tell stories that contain sequential parts. Reading these stories counts, too!

DR. MICHELLE'S TAKEAWAY

THREE-YEAR-OLDS are typically very good at communicating verbally and telling you exactly what they want—and don't want. Expect many grammatical mistakes.

FOUR-YEAR OLDS

By age four, your child's language should be quite developed: He might not have mastered all of English's proper grammar forms, but the basics should be there and he should be a full conversational partner.

Vocabulary

A four-year-old's vocabulary continues to grow and may include more descriptive words and synonyms for words she already knows. For instance, she may say *giggle* in addition to *laugh*.

Pragmatic Language

Four-year-olds will start to use words like *know, think, forget,* and *remember*. While the typical four-year-old speaks very directly, your child should also begin to use indirect requests and sentence constructions such as *I'm hungry*, or *That looks like fun*.

Children this age should begin to feel more comfortable using language as part of their social interaction—speaking with peers, teachers, or perhaps acquaintances they do not see every day. If your child is still somewhat hesitant, that's okay, but if she does not use language at all with her peers, teachers, or caregivers, you should check in with your pediatrician.

Grammar and Sentences

Typical four-year-olds begin to master grammar forms that may have tripped them up at age three, such as many (but not all) of the irregular past tense verbs. Kids this age can conjoin clauses, saying *I ran and fell*, rather than *I ran and I fell*. Their language reflects their cognitive ability to grasp and explain causal relationships: They can correctly use words like *because* or *so*. By this age, children should be able to accurately use a negative construction such as *I don't want milk* (whereas a younger child would simply say *no milk* or *no want milk*).

Somewhere around age four, and for many kids even earlier, kids start to show **metalinguistic skills**. This is the ability to talk about language and verbalize the rules of language. If your child ever said *I don't know the word for that*, then he is showing basic metalinguistic knowledge. Another metalinguistic skill that most four-year-olds can do is rhyming. Don't be concerned if your child has trouble here—it takes lots and lots of practice. Metalinguistic skills are important prerequisites for learning how to read, so keep talking to your four-year-old and keep talking about language—such as calling attention to two words that have the same meaning, like *little* and *small*.

DR. MICHELLE'S TAKEAWAY

FOUR-YEAR-OLDS are effective communicators with adults and peers. Continue to expect grammar mistakes, but correct sentences should be more frequent than those with mistakes.

SCHOOL-AGE CHILDREN

By the time your child enters kindergarten, he has acquired the oral language skills needed to be a successful learner. Remember, children need these skills so they can soon employ them as they learn the mechanics of reading. They can communicate using long sentences and they have mastered the majority of grammar forms. These grammar forms allow them to put together sophisticated ideas, explain events, and talk about the past, present, and future.

Vocabulary

Vocabulary continues to grow during this period, and your school-age child will acquire many of his new words from the classroom. New vocabulary words have richer, more adult-like definitions, and many words reflect school knowledge, including words like *equation, absent, angle, punctuation, hypothesis,* and *definition*. Kids in elementary school appropriately use words like *wish, guess,* and *pretend*. This expanded vocabulary allows them to grasp ideas that are important for storytelling.

Pragmatic Language

Kids in elementary school are effective in using language to communicate with adults and peers. Five- and six-year-olds are able to take into account the listener's perspective when they are speaking, and their language reflects that. So when your six-year-old son is talking about an activity he did over the weekend, he knows his teacher was not present and he provides certain detail about the events accordingly. At age four, your child probably couldn't do this. Conversations no longer focus exclusively on the here and now.

Grammar and Sentences

Some grammar forms continue to be a little tricky. Your child may still say *brung* or *bringed* instead of *brought*, or *swinged* instead of *swung*, for example. Don't fret. Some kids don't master certain irregular forms until they are eight or nine.

Understanding Language

Kids this age start to understand **figurative language**—expressions that mean something other than their literal definition—including metaphors (*It's raining cats and dogs*) and similes (*I'm as hot as the sun*). School-age kids can sometimes understand complex sentence structures, including the passive form such as *The cat was chased by the dog*. The active form of this sentence—the dog chased the cat—is still easier to understand.

The largest area of language growth in early elementary school is in metalinguistic skills. Your child should be able to define words, talking about what is a sound, a letter, a word, and a sentence. As children learn and talk about words, they are able to talk about **synonyms,** words that have the same meaning (like huge and gigantic), and **homophones**, words that sound the same but have different meanings (like bat, the stick used for baseball and the flying animal), as well as the difference between *no* and *know*.

They can also talk about grammar and syntax rules. Elementary schoolchildren can tell you that the sentence *I eated a cookie* is not correct and can explain why is it not correct. These metalinguistic skills are necessary and important for literacy development.

DR. MICHELLE'S TAKEAWAY

LANGUAGE GROWTH ALLOWS children to be successful learners in school. Metalinguistic skills grow as kids enter elementary school. These skills are critical for learning how to read and write.

DR. MICHELLE'S GUIDE TO CHILDREN TELLING A STORY

BEING ABLE TO tell a story using oral language is very important, because oral language skills provide the foundation needed for written language skills. Children who have difficulty with syntax and phonology at two and a half tend to show literacy difficulties in elementary school. Before your child turns two, she can show signs of narrative development by referring to past events (even if she is not using the past tense). These are usually important events in the child's life, like a trip to the beach or an unfortunate accident.

By the time she is three and a half, she should be telling narrative stories that combine two events: *We took the train, and we went to the beach.* Four-year-olds usually tell narratives that contain many events, although they may not necessarily be in the correct order: *We took the train, and went to the beach, and ate ice cream, and went on rides.* Five-year-olds usually get all the events, in the correct order, but may dwell on the climax of the story: *We took the subway train, we went to the beach, we went on rides, and we got ice cream, and mine fell on the floor!*

By the time kids turn six, they can tell a classic narrative that contains appropriate detail, is sequenced correctly, and contains a climax and a resolution: *We took the subway train, we went to the beach, then rode the roller-coaster, and I got mint chocolate chip ice cream. Mine fell on the floor, so I ate Mommy's ice cream.*

 RED FLAGS
What to Look Out For and When

Not all kids master these language milestones right on time. Dr. Michelle has identified nine important red flags that she's noticed over her years as a speech language therapist. Notice that many of these red flags apply to children under two years old, signaling that you can catch many language issues early.

1. Your baby does not respond to his name by 12 months. Babies have been hearing their names since birth, and by the time they are 12 months old—and often earlier—they should consistently respond to their name when it is called. If your child doesn't respond to his name, consider visiting the pediatrician for a hearing check.

2. Your baby does not seem to understand familiar language that is directed at her by 12 months. Babies understand language before they can say words. They should respond to questions like *Where's mama?* and *Where's the ball?* They should also seem to understand phrases and routines like *Wave bye-bye* or *Here's your bottle.*

3. Your baby does not use gestures by 12 months. Babies can be very good communicators before they begin to use words. By the time your baby turns a year old, he should be using gestures like pointing to objects, lifting his arms up to indicate he wants to be picked up, shaking his head no, or waving hi or bye. If he is not using some gestures by this time, you should check in with your pediatrician.

4. Your child does not have a real word by 15 months. Most toddlers say words around their first birthdays. Some say words earlier and some a little later. By 15 months, kids should be saying at least one or two real words. If not, you should bring this up with your pediatrician or regular medical provider.

5. Your child does not say two-word combinations by 24 months. Toddlers start to put words together to form short sentences around the same time they can say 50 words, often starting around 18 months. If your child has not started to do this by her second birthday, it might be time to schedule an evaluation with a speech language therapist.

6. Your child shows regression in language skills at any age. You should notice spurts of language skills in your child; sometimes they will be slow and sometimes fast. But if you observe a loss of skills in any area, definitely check in with your pediatrician.

7. Your three-year-old is unable to refer to past events. She might not have mastered the correct past tense verb form yet, but your three-year-old should have the expressive language skills to talk about past events like a trip or special event. That's an important developmental and cognitive milestone, and it will lead to even more conversational skills later on. Talk to your child's teacher or visit a speech language therapist for an evaluation if you don't notice this milestone.

8. Your four-year-old is unable to chain two events together. He should be able to link two ideas using a conjunction like *and* or a temporal term like *then*. This indicates an ability to join related ideas. Consider an evaluation from a speech language therapist if you don't witness this skill developing.

9. Your six-year-old is unable to sequence events. She should be able to sequence events by stating how things occurred in the correct order. If she's unable to do so, you should check in with her teacher and speak to a speech language therapist.

COMMON QUESTIONS,

EXPERT ANSWERS

Anywhere she goes and meets other parents—whether it's the schoolyard, the grocery store, or the library—Dr. Michelle listens as moms and dads ask questions about how their children are learning and developing their language skills. Here are some of the most common questions that Dr. Michelle hears from parents, and her favorite answers.

QUESTION: *My toddler is 18 months old and she's not saying any words. Should I be concerned?*

ANSWER: Maybe. The majority of babies begin saying words around their first birthday and have around 50 words at 18 months. It's possible that your toddler is a late talker or that she has a developmental language delay (terms that we'll define later in this chapter). Or it's possible that she needs her hearing checked out.

QUESTION: *What is baby sign language and will it improve my baby's language skills?*

ANSWER: Baby sign language is when babies with typical hearing are taught to use certain gestures to represent words, such as *please, give me, milk,* or *more,* before they can verbalize them. In the short run, baby sign language can help your little one communicate better with you. But there is no scientific evidence that shows these kids have larger verbal vocabularies later on than babies who were not taught baby signs.

QUESTION: *Is it true that girls are more talkative than boys?*

ANSWER: According to scientific research, yes! Initially, girls say more words. Language specialists including Larry Fenson and Elizabeth Bates and their colleagues have been collecting information about how many words kids acquire at different ages into a huge database called the MacArthur-Bates Communicative Development Inventories. According to research relying on some of this data, at 18 months old, the average girl says 104 words and the average boy can say 85 words. At 24 months, girls have average vocabularies of 346 words; boys, 252. Linguists are still grappling with why these discrepancies exist. Researchers have detected gender differences in how adults direct their language to children. Adults are likely to refer to girls as sweetie and honey and boys as buddy and big guy, and speak to them with different vocabularies and about different topics.

QUESTION: *You've said we should talk to our babies a lot. Does* Sesame Street *count?*

ANSWER: No, no, and no. We mean you—or another living human—should talk to your baby. Academic research shows that babies do not acquire language from watching television (or, ahem, using a phone or tablet) the same way they do from interacting with a human voice. The American Academy of Pediatrics recommends that children under age two not watch television or be exposed to other screen time.

We know that TV can provide you or your child a break. We've used it, too. But your child is not acquiring language from screen time.

QUESTION: *My first child was an early talker and my second child seems to be a little bit delayed. Is that normal?*

ANSWER: Yes. Children born second (and third and fourth) tend to meet language milestones a little later than firstborn children. By later, Dr. Michelle means a delay of about one to two months. Firstborn children tend to produce words earlier because they receive more attention and hear more child-directed speech; younger children, however, have to compete with other family members. So if your firstborn child said his first word at 11 months, you should not be surprised if your second-born says his first word at 13 months—but if you are not hearing any words by 15 months, you would want to check in with your pediatrician.

QUESTION: *My child says* brung *instead of* brought *and* builded *instead of* built. *Can I correct her?*

ANSWER: It depends how old she is. If she's less than five, not yet—kids learn grammar through modeling, or hearing the proper speech and language from adults. When they have begun to master metalinguistic skills (as discussed previously), adults can draw attention to their language. So, for a child over age five, you might gently call attention to the difference between a correct and incorrect use of a word. But we have also learned the hard way that children don't love to be nagged!

A COMMON CONCERN: LATE TALKERS

While many children display variations in their language development, Dr. Michelle urges you to check in with a speech language therapist or pediatrician if your child shows any of the red flags described here in Chapter 3. But let's now discuss the most common concern for children with language delays.

Late talkers is a term speech and language professionals use to describe children who show typical development in motor, cognitive, hearing, and social and behavioral milestones, but have delays in language. A late talker is usually defined as a child of 24 months who says fewer than 50 words and does not combine words. As a point of comparison, a typical 24-month-old says 300 words and combines words into two-, three-, and four-word sentences.

Late talkers are very common; it is estimated that 15 to 20 percent of toddlers are late talkers. Late talking is more common in boys than in girls and is more common in families with histories of language delay or difficulties.

Dr. Michelle has done some important research in this area and has found that many late talkers show delays in their ability to say speech sounds, too. Kids who are late talkers were also often late babblers, so they didn't get all the practice they needed in saying their speech sounds. Practice saying speech sounds via babble is a very important skill needed to build vocabulary words. **So there can be a correlation between a late talker's speech sounds and later language (and even reading) skills.**

Research shows that many late talkers—somewhere between 50 and 75 percent of these kids—**grow out of the delay and show average language skills by the time they enter kindergarten.** Kids who seem to recover from their delay are often labeled **late bloomers**. But even these kids do not totally catch up completely—their language skills, although average, are not the same as their peers who did not have an early language delay. A very important longitudinal study by clinical developmental psychologist Leslie Rescorla and colleagues followed a group of late talkers from 24 months to 17 years. Their language and literacy skills were tested every year or every couple of years and compared to a group of children who did not have an early language delay. The majority of the late talkers in these studies showed language skills in the average range by the time they entered kindergarten, but significantly lower than their peers at every age tested through high school.

Early language is important for later academic success. That's why Dr. Michelle is a big advocate for seeking an evaluation from a speech language therapist if you think your child may be a late talker or is even on the cusp. Keep monitoring your child as he progresses through preschool and early elementary school, and **work especially hard at home in getting your child to master his language skills—** for your child, language acquisition may simply take more practice. Kids who are late talkers may be at risk for other developmental and behavioral disorders, such as **language impairment (LI)**, an umbrella term for slow language development in typically developing children. (We will discuss these other language-related concerns in greater length in Chapter 7, along with autism spectrum disorders and certain attention and learning disorders. And we will provide you with more ways to seek help in Chapter 8.)

SOME SIMPLE THINGS TO DO AT HOME

Whatever path your child is on, every parent can do more to help their child's language skills to blossom and develop so their vocabulary grows and their sentence structure sounds more adultlike. Here are Dr. Michelle's top tips.

BABIES

Talk to your baby. Talk a lot. Read to her. As we mentioned earlier, **there is a direct correlation between how much time a caregiver**

spends speaking to a child and the child's language skills later on. Be sure that when talking to your baby, you look into her eyes. And respond when your baby vocalizes. You are teaching your baby important pragmatic language rules. What should you talk about with your baby?

- **Everyday routines.** Talk about what is going on around her. When you give her a bath, talk about her body parts, and when you get her dressed talk about her clothes.
- **Events that will happen.** Talk about upcoming events, such as a visit with grandparents or a birthday party, and who will be there and what will happen.
- **Events that have happened.** Talk about who was at the event and what happened.

TODDLERS AND PRESCHOOLERS

Keep talking to your two-, three-, and four-year-olds. They are listening and want to talk to you. Also, sing, clap, dance, and wiggle. Kids love music, repetition, and rhyme. You may be sick of "Twinkle, Twinkle, Little Star" or "The Wheels on the Bus," but your child is not. Believe it or not, music, rhyme, and repetition provide important preliteracy skills. Here are some other tricks to get your kids talking:

- Rather than asking yes or no questions, give choices: *Do you want apples or bananas?*
- Ask open-ended questions that start with *Tell me about* . . . rather than *What's that?* Open-ended questions allow children to respond using more complex sentences as compared to questions that require one-word responses.
- Play, talk, and **pause** when interacting with your child. The last part—pausing—is important. We are good at playing and talking, but sometimes adults can dominate a conversation. Give your child an opportunity to respond.

KINDERGARTEN TO FOURTH GRADE

Your child's oral language skills can have a big impact on her reading and writing skills. Work with your child to encourage her metalinguistic skills.

○ Talk about definitions of words, especially words that have multiple meanings.

○ Continue to ask open-ended questions and pause. Listen carefully for your child's response. You can use phrases like, *I wonder what would happen if . . .* or *What do you think will happen next?* and *Tell me why you think that.*

○ Talk about things that are important to your child. Children will be motivated to talk about (and learn more about) topics that they are interested in.

RESOURCES

We know how tempting it is to take to the internet to find out about whether your child is meeting his milestones, what other parents are saying about their kids' language development, and how you can generally be an even better parent than you are. But Dr. Michelle is a big fan of research-based sites about language development. Here are some of her favorite sites:

○ The American Speech-Language-Hearing Association (ASHA), the primary professional organization of licensed and certified speech language therapists, has a page about milestones for language (and speech and hearing) development: *http://www.asha.org/public/speech/development/chart/*.
  • ASHA also has a great page about the social conventions of language: *http://www.asha.org/public/speech/development/Pragmatics/*.

○ The National Institutes of Health, the federal agency that provides research on health matters, has a handy checklist of language development: *http://www.nidcd.nih.gov/health/voice/pages/speechandlanguage.aspx.*

○ If you are interested in a very in-depth, data-driven site about how children in many different countries acquire language, check out the website for the MacArthur-Bates Communicative Development Inventories (CDIs), housed at Stanford University: *http://mb-cdi.stanford.edu.*

4

FLUENCY

Making Speech and Language Sound Smooth

I N PREVIOUS CHAPTERS, we explored the foundations for developing oral language. In Chapter 2, we focused on speech—the physical and motor movements needed to produce sounds and syllables and words and sentences. Then, in Chapter 3, we gave you a little primer on language—a system of symbols, such as spoken words, sounds, and sentences, used to represent things like objects, events, people, and ideas. But your brain must figure out how to put its speech skills and its language skills together. It must be able to deliver those sounds and words with the right speed, with the appropriate number of breaks and pauses, and in a way that is easily understood by listeners. Speech language professionals call this **fluency**.

In this chapter, we will explain what fluency is and why it's crucial for all kids to develop. We will also examine the typical issues that may arise as your child develops her ability to speak fluently, and walk you through any issues that may require a bit more attention.

WHAT'S FLUENCY, ANYWAY?

Fluency is the effortless and forward flow of speech. Someone who speaks fluently does so in a manner that is smooth and without difficulty.

Fluency is an important oral language skill for all children. Fluent speech helps them to be effective communicators. In Chapter 3, we explained that children often speak first, and exclusively, to their parents, caregivers, and siblings. However, as they grow older, typically starting around age three or a bit after, they begin to address a wide range of listeners, from their peers to their teachers, relatives, acquaintances, their friends' parents, and perhaps even a school principal. They use language in a range of settings: at the playground, in the classroom, at a restaurant, or at a family gathering. **Kids need to communicate, and fluency helps them to achieve this essential skill.**

We may all aspire to achieve fluency consistently, but it's not an all-or-nothing goal. Neither children nor adults speak fluently 100 percent of the time. Often, when we begin speaking, we lose our train of thought, stop or struggle to think of a word, and use filler words or expressions such as *um*, *like*, and *ya know* until the word we are searching for comes to mind. Articulating a complex sentence or idea can take more effort than a simple one. Everyone, even world leaders, will stumble on their words or hesitate to find them at times. When Barack Obama was campaigning to be president in 2008, David Letterman broadcast a segment on his show called the "Barack Obama uh count," tallying how many *uhs* he uttered during a media blitz.

Fluency is a two-pronged skill. Think of it as speech + language = fluency. Remember, as we discussed in Chapter 2, kids need to coordinate all their motor skills and their cognitive skills to produce speech sounds. Your child needs to be able to integrate his speech production skills—respiration, phonation, and articulation—while simultaneously planning his language output—what he is going to say. Putting this all together can be quite complicated. It is not something people are typically conscious of. And when kids are using both their speech and language skills to communicate a complex idea, or when language skills are more advanced than motor skills, fluency can suffer.

Fluency can be a bit of a roller-coaster for kids. One day your child's speech may be perfectly smooth; the next, you'll begin wondering why he is using words like *uh* or *um*, or repeating words or syllables in his sentences. These fluctuations can occur depending on the social setting, the number of listeners, the time of day, or the discussion topic at hand.

When your child begins putting words together, typically sometime before his second birthday, you may begin to notice his fluency development as well. **There is huge variation in the fluency patterns of typically developing children.** Some kids begin speaking in a manner that is smooth, only occasionally veering from that, and yet other kids struggle greatly to say certain words and to combine words to make sentences. This is true even if these kids are acquiring all their speech sounds and developing their language at the expected time. As they develop their crucial oral language skills from eighteen months to five years, most kids fall somewhere in the middle of the fluency spectrum. Most of the time that your child is speaking, he should demonstrate enough fluency to be an effective communicator.

DR. MICHELLE'S TAKEAWAY

SPEECH FLUENCY VARIES greatly in typically developing children, especially when they are excited, tired, or expressing complex ideas.

WHAT'S HAPPENING WHEN SPEECH IS NOT SMOOTH?

So we know how we all want to talk—perfectly smoothly. And we know how we actually talk—with a lack of perfect smoothness.

Speech professionals refer to a bump, or repetition, in our speech as a **disfluency** (also spelled **dysfluency**)—an interruption in a smooth flow of speech.

All speakers, young and old, experience disfluencies. In adults, disfluencies often work like this: We start a sentence, then stop; we can't think of a word, so we use an interjection such as *like, um*, or *you know*. We may do this several times as we're talking. You probably notice that some grown-ups do this a lot.

You might notice something a little different in your child, though. Children have more instances of disfluencies as compared to adults, and these disfluencies tend to be sound and word repetitions. **It's very common for children to demonstrate disfluencies when they are acquiring language, all the while trying to perfect their speech sounds. Experts refer to these common disfluencies in young children as normal disfluencies.**

The milestones for fluency development aren't set in stone. But we know that there's a strong correlation between the rapid language development that takes place when kids are in their early preschool years and the incidence of disfluencies that parents and caregivers hear in kids' speech. These disfluencies tend to peak when a child is two to three and a half years old, and then diminish over time, gradually tapering off somewhere around four or five.

You may find that your child goes through a period of disfluency for a phase of a few days or weeks and then, suddenly, her fluency may seem greatly improved. Or you may notice that she shows disfluency during certain social situations, such as when she's talking to a teacher or a friend's parent. She may have an easier time telling you that she wants a cookie than telling a long story about what happened yesterday on the playground. Remember, saying a long sentence requires coordinating both her speech sounds and her developing storytelling skills. That's a lot of work. If you become aware of a lot of disfluency, think about whether something has changed in her world. Did a new sibling come along? Did you move? Did your child start a new daycare or preschool program? These big life events can all affect her fluency.

Here are some examples of **normal disfluencies** that you may hear:

○ **Revisions**, when a child gets midway through a word and then decides to use another one, such as *That ice cream is bi . . . it's huge* or *I want straw . . . vanilla ice cream.*

○ **Interjections**, when a child adds a filler word such as *uh or um* into his sentence, such as *I um, um, want a turn.*

○ **Repetitions**, when a child repeats a syllable or word, such as *Mom-mom, I want that* or *It's a-a-a hippopotamus.* These repetitions often occur at the beginning of a phrase or sentence; it's sort of like your child is just revving up her speech engine.

And here's how frequently you may hear these disfluencies:

○ One to two units of disfluency at a time, such as *That's my-my ball,* or *Mom-mom, where's the dinosaur?*

○ No more than 10 disfluencies per 100 spoken words.

PARENTING TIP

WHEN DR. MICHELLE evaluates children to observe their fluency patterns, she records them so she can count the frequency of disfluencies in their speech. Not every parent can count how many repetitions they hear in every 100 words! So if you are concerned about your child's disfluency, take out your phone and make a recording of your child speaking a few sentences or telling a story, and then review it when your child is not around, counting the frequency of disfluencies in the context of the overall number of words she says.

Your child's disfluencies might sound striking to you, but here's some good news: Children who show normal disfluencies are typically not bothered by them and show little or no frustration when speaking; the disfluencies we described simply aren't noticeable to a three- or four-year-old. Some more good news is that other listeners do not typically respond negatively to these occasional repetitions and stops and starts. You may notice that when your child speaks with some disfluencies, adults such as parents, teachers, or relatives will listen patiently as he speaks. As for your child's peers, they tend not to notice these disfluencies at all.

DR. MICHELLE'S TAKEAWAY

EXPECT NORMAL DISFLUENCIES, especially during periods of rapid language growth, between 1½ and 5 years of age.

LET'S LOOK AT STUTTERING

Some disfluencies are different from others. While kids ages one and a half to five often show quite a bit of normal disfluency (peaking at around age three), others demonstrate signs of a more atypical disfluency—early **stuttering**. Stuttering is when a speaker's speech is disrupted and does not flow smoothly. (Occasionally, you might hear the term **stammering**, which refers to the same condition. However, clinical researchers and speech language therapists in the United States don't tend to use that term anymore, although it may be used in other parts of the English-speaking world.)

Stuttering is considered a speech motor disorder because it means that kids have a hard time coordinating all the different aspects of speech production—such as respiration and phonation—to speak effortlessly. When it is first observed in childhood, it is referred to as **developmental stuttering**, meaning that it evolves during the period of speech and language acquisition.

There is a subspecialty of speech and language research devoted specifically to studying disfluencies and stuttering. Many of the most important studies and research advances in this area have been made by professional linguists and speech language therapists who themselves stutter or stuttered as children. They have studied the mechanics of stuttering, its causes, and the best therapies for addressing it.

A major pioneer in the study of stuttering, and the development of key therapies for treating it, was Charles Van Riper, a speech language therapist who himself stuttered and developed some of the foundational research about stuttering starting in the 1930s. One of his main contributions to the field was an identification of what he labeled **core behaviors** of stuttering, or **behaviors frequently seen in people who stutter and that are considered different from the normal disfluencies that occur in everyday speech.**

These core behaviors include:

- ○ Repetitions of:
    - Sounds (such as *b-b-b-b-us*)
    - Syllables (such as *ele-ele-ele-phant*)
    - Words (such as *The-the-the-the bus is coming!*)
- ○ **Prolongations**, or saying a sound with a longer duration than usual, as in the names *Sssssssssam, Lllllllily,* or *Rrrrrryan*
- ○ **Blocks**, or the stoppage of airflow during speech, which sounds like someone is stuck when speaking or struggling for air or holding their breath

Individuals who stutter also show the other types of disfluencies—the hesitations or pauses, interjections (e.g., *um, like, uh, ya know*), or rephrasing or revising of a word, phrase, or sentence that are observed in normally disfluent kids. **But individuals who stutter may use these types of disfluencies more often than those who are normally disfluent.**

BORDERLINE STUTTERING

Sometimes children show signs of normal disfluency along with signs of true stuttering. Specialists refer to this as **borderline stuttering**, a kind of speech that is somewhere in between normal disfluency and full-blown stuttering. Barry Guitar, a professor of communication sciences at the University of Vermont and a stutterer himself, has done detailed research to show how children progress from one stage of disfluency to another.

Some days a child may appear to be normally disfluent, while other days fluency is more difficult. Some kids just work through it; other kids show persistent difficulties with fluency. **Some kids who show borderline stuttering around ages two to five grow out of it and, by the time they are in kindergarten, have the same fluency levels as their peers. Other kids with borderline stuttering progress to other stages of stuttering,** which we will discuss later in this chapter.

You probably want to know how you can tell if your child is demonstrating normal disfluency or borderline stuttering. Because fluency varies considerably in children, it can be hard to determine. **A child who shows borderline stuttering demonstrates the characteristics of normal disfluency but exhibits them more frequently than other children.** Some children go through a period where they go back and forth between normal disfluency and borderline stuttering, while others progress to show signs of early stuttering. Typically, these children do not show signs of frustration or awareness of disfluencies. **If your child seems to be getting frustrated when he stutters, then you should keep monitoring him and schedule an evaluation with a speech language therapist if his stuttering continues to progress.**

If you think your child is showing signs of borderline stuttering, you should count how often you hear disfluencies from her. Try to use a simple video recorder, like one on a phone, to record your child speaking and tally up her disfluencies; you might have to revisit the recording a few times, but it could help you understand how frequently disfluencies occur. Remember, two signs of normal disfluency are word repetitions that are fewer than 10 per 100 words, and one or two units of disfluency at a time. By contrast, signs of borderline stuttering include repetitions of sounds, syllables, and words as well as sound prolongations that are:

- ○ More than 10 disfluencies per 100 spoken words
- ○ Three or more units of disfluency at a time (e.g., That's *my-my-my* ball!)

DR. MICHELLE'S TAKEAWAY

SOME KIDS FLUCTUATE between normal disfluency and stuttering. If your child exhibits this pattern, monitor your child's fluency for six to eight weeks and schedule an evaluation with a speech language therapist if the stuttering progresses.

WHAT'S THE DIFFERENCE?

SINCE NEARLY ALL young children from one and a half to five years of age show signs of disfluency, it can be hard to distinguish between normal disfluency and stuttering. Dr. Michelle has listened to hundreds of young children and tries to help parents determine when their speech is considered to have normal disfluencies and when they are borderline stuttering.

Take the example of Max and Sam. They are both four-year-olds and it's their first day of preschool and their teacher asks them a few questions.

Teacher: Good morning, boys and girls. Please tell us your name.

Max: My name is-is Max.

Sam: My-my-my name is Sssssam.

Teacher: Now, boys and girls, please share with the class what you did during your summer vacation.

Max: This summer I, um, went to the beach and I, um, rode my bike in the park.

Sam: This summer I-I-I-I, um, I don't know.

We can tell that Max is showing signs of normal disfluency because he used word repetitions and interjections that involved one or two units. Sam seems to be a borderline stutterer because he showed three and four units of repetition as well as a prolongation.

STUTTERING IN THE EARLY YEARS OF CHILDHOOD

Some children who show borderline stuttering progress to a more severe form of stuttering. Sometimes, this stuttering is an evolution of the disfluencies that began before age five, when they were acquiring most of their language skills, whereas in some other kids stuttering seems to begin out of the blue, during elementary school or even high school—although this is more rare. The greatest incidence of stuttering begins in early childhood.

You may notice a child of around five years of age or older beginning to show more instances of sound, syllable, and word repetitions. That child might also be showing lots of **sound prolongations**—again, when a regular sound is stretched out, particularly when the first sound of a syllable is said. **A child demonstrating signs of beginning stuttering may also be blocking on words, meaning his articulators seem to be stuck.**

There is another component that comes into play with early stuttering: The child who is beginning to stutter becomes aware of his disfluencies. He may anticipate stuttering on a certain word because he has had trouble saying it before and is anxious he will start stuttering again. Your child may not say, "Mom, I can't get my word out," but he may tell you in other ways, such as showing you that he is frustrated, stressed, or scared. This is your child telling you, *Speaking is not so easy for me.*

Your child may exhibit what speech language professionals call **secondary behaviors**, or learned behaviors that people who stutter do in order to get through their anxieties of having disfluent speech. **Typically, once kids are aware of their stuttering and try to control it, they begin to show these secondary behaviors, which is why self-awareness of disfluencies is a very important milestone in the progression of stuttering.**

One way in which your child may show secondary behaviors is with **avoidance behaviors**, which are actions children take to not stutter. She may avoid saying particular words or phrases she knows she might stutter on, or try to avoid speaking situations when she thinks she may stutter. She may not raise her hand to speak in class. She may not want to socialize with kids who make her nervous or stressed, for fear of stuttering.

Another way your child may show secondary behaviors is with **escape behaviors**, which are actions that people who stutter take to get out of the stuttering event while it is happening. He may nod his head, blink his eyes, or stomp his feet while he stutters. His lips may tremble.

Many young children who stutter are not aware they are disfluent, especially when they first begin stuttering. But over time, especially when children are particularly disfluent, they may become frustrated when speaking. And because speech and language are interactive, listeners may begin to respond differently when they speak and are disfluent. Listeners may not maintain eye contact, or they may fill in words for the child, or they may lose attention. Kids can pick up on these stressful situations, which may lead, in turn, to their feeling even more anxious or inadequate when they speak.

Your child's feelings and attitudes toward speaking contribute to his ability to be a successful communicator in many kinds of settings.

If he is fearful of stuttering, he can be fearful of talking in general, which can affect his ability to communicate, especially in situations like talking on the phone or being in groups, at restaurants, or in a noisy classroom.

If you do notice your child stuttering frequently, she is not alone. Researchers estimate that about 5 percent of preschoolers and about one percent of school-age children stutter. About one percent of the general population experiences persistent stuttering.

WHAT CAUSES STUTTERING?

Researchers have not determined definitively what causes stuttering, but we do know certain facts about developmental stuttering that may help explain why it develops in some kids and not others, and why certain kids are more predisposed to stuttering than others.

- **Stuttering runs in families.** Scientists think that some people are born with certain genetic traits that predispose them to stutter. Researchers from the National Institutes of Health have identified three specific genes that seem to be responsible for stuttering. Stuttering does not necessarily manifest itself in all children with these genetic predispositions; usually a life event can trigger difficulties with fluency. The triggers may be learning the rules of grammar, or a stressful situation like the arrival of a new sibling, or a move to a new house.
- **Stuttering occurs more frequently in boys than girls.** Among preschoolers who stutter, there are about twice as many boys as girls. Girls are more likely to recover from stuttering early, so among school-age children, four times as many boys as girls stutter.
- **Stuttering is usually observed when speech and language are being acquired rapidly.**
- **Stuttering can be brought on by an environmental trigger.** For example:

- When major life events occur, such as a new sibling, a move, a death of a family member, or a divorce. It's important to understand that these events do not cause stuttering, but may affect a child's fluency.
- When a child is being asked to perform, such as when the parent says, "Tommy, tell grandma what we did yesterday."
- When children are being hurried.
- When children feel a loss of listener attention from adults or peers.
- When there is a lot of competition for speaking, such as from other siblings at home or other children in the classroom.

○ **Occasionally, stuttering occurs because of a known neurologic condition.** If a child has a stroke or a tumor, areas of the brain that affect smooth, fluent speech can be affected. This kind of stuttering is called **acquired stuttering** or **neurogenic stuttering**, and it is more typical in adults than children.

FROM RESEARCH TO REAL LIFE

MANY CHILDREN WHO stutter in their early years recover while they're still relatively young. Researchers are still trying to determine exactly why some kids recover and others need more help. Some kids recover spontaneously, meaning without therapies, while others need therapy to help promote fluency. A large-scale study conducted by University of Illinois professors Ehud Yairi and Nicoline Grinager Ambrose, published in 1999, found that about 75 percent of children who stuttered as preschoolers—the average age of participants being a little over three years old—recovered spontaneously, or without treatment, and 25 percent were persistent stutterers. It took some kids six months to recover, and others, several years. About 25 percent of preschool children who stutter will continue to stutter in elementary, middle, and high school, and some into adulthood, these researchers concluded. Researchers are not sure why some children recover while others don't. It is likely that unique genetic, biological, environmental, and personality factors in each child contribute to their fluency (and disfluency).

Today, current research focuses on using neuroimaging technology to determine what goes on in the brain when people stutter—research that ultimately could help kids who do not recover from stuttering on their own.

 RED FLAGS
What to Look Out For and When

As we've said, it's hard to know just what causes stuttering. Sometimes it's even difficult for experts to determine when normal disfluencies give way to borderline or early stuttering. Dr. Michelle believes that these five red flags can help you identify if your child might need an evaluation from a speech language therapist to assess whether his speech patterns are typical for his age. Remember that you may see many of these red flags during or after a major life change—such as a divorce, the arrival of a new sibling, a change in school, or the death of a family member or pet.

1. If there is a family history of stuttering. A child who has a parent, aunt, or uncle who stutters is much more predisposed to stutter as well.

2. If your child makes sound, syllable, or word repetitions that are more than three units at a time. Repeating sounds, syllables, or words is quite common in young children, but if these repetitions are more than three units, such as *My-my-my-my name is Sue*, then you should monitor your child closely. If the repetitions persist for more than three months, check in with a speech language therapist.

3. If your child seems frustrated or discouraged during failed communication attempts. This is a sign that your child is gaining awareness of his disfluency, and it is time to check in with a speech language therapist to help him handle his disfluencies and his discomfort.

4. If your child shows blocks, or seems to stop or get stuck at the beginning or middle of words and seems to be gasping for breath, then you will definitely want to speak with a speech language therapist.

5. If you notice your child exhibiting any secondary behaviors related to his disfluencies, such as avoiding certain words or speaking situations or showing physical characteristics when speaking, like head nods or hard eye blinks, then you want to contact a speech language therapist immediately.

COMMON QUESTIONS,
EXPERT ANSWERS

Parents of young children often ask Dr. Michelle to listen to their child's speech patterns because it can be so hard for untrained professionals to determine if children are showing normal fluency or a type of more full-blown stuttering. Here are the questions she hears most frequently from parents, and her informed answers:

QUESTION: *My five-year-old stumbles over a particular word. Is this normal?*

ANSWER: Probably. Some words are tricky for kids, especially words with many syllables like *cinnamon*, *spaghetti*, or *hibernation*. It may take several tries to say words like these correctly and fluently. However, if your child is getting stuck on a word that he says often, like his name or the name of a good friend, then he may be showing something more than normal disfluency.

QUESTION: *My child seems to stutter all the time. Will he grow out of it?*

ANSWER: He may. About 5 percent of children go through a period of stuttering and one percent of children show persistent stuttering, so many kids do outgrow periods of disfluency. But some kids need extra help in outgrowing this tendency, so if you observe any of the red flags as listed in this chapter, then Dr. Michelle suggests you check in with a speech language therapist who specializes in stuttering to determine if your child is showing signs of normal disfluency or stuttering.

QUESTION: *My husband's sister used to stutter as a child. Should I worry about my child?*

ANSWER: Possibly. We do know that stuttering runs in families, so if your family has a positive history, then it is a good idea to listen carefully to your child's speech and consider your child at-risk.

QUESTION: *My child stutters. Will he fall behind in school?*

ANSWER: Fluency can have a correlation with school performance. Research shows that children who stutter may show difficulties with language acquisition and school performance, as compared to children who don't stutter. But researchers don't know exactly why this correlation exists. A child's school performance may be related to his stuttering and the social effects of it. For example, some kids may respond "I don't know" to a teacher's question—even if he knows the answer—because he does not want to express the answer verbally for fear of being disfluent. Or he may not want to participate in classroom discussion. But studies regarding whether there is an underlying language weakness that affects academic performance in children who stutter are still inconclusive.

QUESTION: *Did I cause my child's stuttering?*

ANSWER: No. Parents don't cause stuttering. The unique genetic makeup of, and developmental and environmental influences on, your child has influenced his ability to speak smoothly. Although you did not cause your child's stuttering, you can do a lot to help her speak more fluently, such as by modeling a slow, easy way of speaking and giving your child plenty of time to respond to questions. (We'll give more tips on how you can aid your child at home later in this chapter.)

A PARENT'S PERSPECTIVE

Russell's Story

Russell was about three years old when his mom and dad noticed that he would repeat the same words when he would start a sentence—sometimes more than five times at once. They weren't sure if they should seek an evaluation from a speech language therapist, but one thing tipped off his mom: Russell started showing signs of frustration when he couldn't get his words out. He would grow quite upset and cry. Russell's parents took him for an evaluation with a speech language therapist, who recommended therapy not only for stuttering, but also for other language delays that were identified during the evaluation. He now receives therapy for stuttering as well as other speech and language delays. While the stuttering has not completely gone away, Russell now pauses before saying words—sometimes a long pause—but he rarely gets stuck on his words.

A tip from Russell's parents: Frustration with stuttering can be one way to distinguish normal disfluency from early stuttering. When Russell had frequent tantrums from his word blocks, his mom knew it was time to check in with a speech language therapist.

TREATMENT FOR STUTTERING

Here's some good news: There is treatment for stuttering. Stuttering research is a subspecialty, and one of the things these researchers specialize in is determining the best methods for treatment, depending on the child's age, the severity of the stuttering, and its duration.

If you are concerned about your child's fluency, **be sure to seek an evaluation and treatment from a speech language therapist who specializes in this area.** (The resources at the end of this chapter will help you find someone who has an expertise in stuttering.) As part of an evaluation, expect a therapist to observe your child's speech while he is speaking in a variety of situations. The therapist may observe your child while he is playing, while he looks at pictures and names objects, and while he tells a story out loud. If he is reading, the therapist may listen to him read a book aloud. She may even ask you to bring in a video from home to determine if your child is showing signs of normal disfluency or stuttering at home.

Treatment for stuttering may vary significantly depending on whether your child is considered to have borderline stuttering, mild stuttering, or severe stuttering. Age matters, too: The protocol will be different if a child is four years old or if she is eight. For a younger child, for example, treatment may involve playing games with speech, such as speaking *slow like a snail* or *fast like a rabbit*, but an older child may be more aware that he is receiving therapy and the therapy may be centered on calling his attention to his speech. **Keep in mind that stuttering can take months or years to treat**.

There are many strategies to help a child with his stuttering. A speech language therapist will likely teach your child the difference between disfluent speech, which a therapist may call **bumpy speech** when talking with children, and fluent speech, which is often referred to as **smooth speech** when working with your child. The therapist may work with an older child to help him understand how often he repeats a particular sound or syllable. She will also work with your child to teach him strategies to achieve fluent speech. These strategies may include reducing your child's rate of speech, helping him to talk slower, and easing him into the first sounds in words, called an **easy onset**. In addition to improving speech fluency, a speech language therapist will also work with your child on reducing secondary behaviors by helping him identify, understand, and control these behaviors.

Treatment for stuttering can take place at home as well. A speech language therapist who specializes in stuttering will discuss treatment that parents and other primary caregivers can help out with. **Working on stuttering requires full family involvement**. Your child's speech language therapist should work with you and your child's primary caregivers on how to respond to your child's disfluencies. The therapist may recommend that you point them out to your child by saying something like, "You said that using bumpy speech. Now try again using smooth speech." Or the therapist may recommend that you *not* bring attention to your child's disfluencies. These recommendations may vary depending on the age of your child and the severity of his stuttering.

In addition, your child's therapist may help educate the family about stuttering and recommend adjustments to daily activities and routines. The therapist may make a home visit (or several visits) to learn about the child's home environment and what kind of dialogue takes place there. The therapist may offer tips on how to create a relaxed and slower pace to help improve your child's fluency. Or you may be advised on how to model a slow, easy way of speaking and encouraged to make sure you always listen to your child and show you are listening by maintaining eye contact, or to find ways to reduce competition for attention and talking in the home.

Finally, the therapist might help educate the child's teachers about his stuttering. School can be very stressful for a child who stutters, as well as for his teachers. A good therapist can come up with some strategies to help your child, such as letting him choose when he has a turn to talk in the classroom, rather than waiting to be called on out of the blue.

SOME SIMPLE THINGS TO DO AT HOME

For all children, but especially for those who stutter, try to make your home a relaxed place to feel comfortable talking. We're parents, too, and we know how hard it is to keep things calm, especially when you are rushing in the morning to go to work or school, or when you're cooking dinner while also trying to help a child with homework and cleaning up the toys strewn throughout your house. These situations can be stressful for kids—we know that they are stressful for adults—and one way that young children express this stress is through their speech fluency. So Dr. Michelle suggests some ways to keep your home environment calm so that your child can feel comfortable speaking and expressing her ideas in it:

○ Speak in a slow and easy manner.
○ Give your child time to respond; wait, look your son or daughter in the eye, and listen.

○ Do not rush your child when she is speaking.

○ Be sure everyone in the family has a turn talking.

○ Try not to fill in words for your child; give him time to complete his thought or sentence.

○ Communicate your strategies for working on your child's fluency to all of your child's caregivers. Make sure everyone has a similar plan.

A tip from Russell's parents: Working on one child's fluency is a family affair. When Russell began stuttering, his sisters would make fun of him and interrupt him. His parents had to work with each sibling to make sure they were giving everyone a chance to talk.

RESOURCES

A host of websites provide information for parents who are wondering about the smoothness of their child's speech, as well as those who are learning more about stuttering and how they can help their children's disfluencies. Here are some of the sites that Dr. Michelle finds most informative and trustworthy:

○ The American Speech-Language-Hearing Association (ASHA) provides general information about stuttering. Go to the ASHA's Find a Professional link to search for a speech language therapist that specializes in stuttering: *http://www. asha.org/public/speech/disorders/stuttering.*

○ The National Stuttering Association is a self-help group for people who stutter, as well as their parents and caregivers: *http://www.nsastutter.org/.*

○ The Stuttering Foundation of America provides free online resources for people who stutter and their families: *http:// www.stutteringhelp.org/.*

○ Phil Schneider, a speech-language pathologist who specializes in fluency disorders, produced a moving and informative documentary that follows individuals who stutter. It can be seen at: *http://www.schneiderspeech.com/media/*.

○ The Stuttering Center of Western Pennsylvania provides helpful information about stuttering: *http://www.stuttering center.org/index.htm*.

5

LITERACY

Reading Begins with Talking

W AIT, YOU MAY be thinking. I thought I bought a book about talking! Why is Dr. Michelle suddenly telling me about reading?

Actually, oral language is the foundation for **literacy**, the ability to read and write. So when your baby starts babbling and jargoning, he is laying the groundwork not only for his language skills—his ability to, one day, speak in entire sentences—but also for his reading and writing skills—his ability to, one day, read and write an entire sentence (or more).

Researchers have shown that, in general, there is a positive correlation between oral language and written language: Kids who are good talkers also tend to become good readers and writers. (But don't worry, because even if your three-year-old hasn't always talked up a storm, he can still be an A+ reader as he grows older.) There are other factors, too, that can contribute to a child's literacy successes. We will discuss these factors and expose you to the various elements of literacy in this chapter.

We'll identify literacy stages and explain how they are influenced by oral language skills—from how those first words influence the ability to read and write, to the early pre-reading abilities of a toddler, to the demands and challenges of the middle-grade reader. We'll walk you through the beginning stages of writing, too. We'll also give you a list of red flags to look out for that can be early-warning signs of reading troubles and explore a common concern regarding children who have difficulties learning to read. Finally, we will discuss how you can help your child become a better reader, from the books you choose to read to your two-year-old to the way you read with your six-year-old.

WHAT ARE THE ELEMENTS OF LITERACY?

Many elements go into the ability to read and write. Reading involves gaining meaning from print. This includes using a written alphabet, developing the ability to translate letters into sounds and words, and using oral language to understand a message. Reading is really important: **Researchers have over many years found a strong correlation between reading skills and academic success.**

And the ability to read springs from the ability to talk. Oral communication helps foster literacy. When you talk and read to your child—even a child as young as 6 months—you are imbuing him with vital skills that will nurture his literacy development. That's because many of the fundamental elements of literacy are born from oral language skills. As kids acquire language skills, their vocabulary knowledge helps them learn what words mean. They gain **syntactic knowledge**—knowledge of how words combine to form phrases and sentences, and knowledge of grammar, such as word endings and noun-verb agreement. The oral language skills your child develops when she is 3 and 4 are ones she will directly transfer to reading. Her storytelling abilities, such as her ability to talk about past events, will enable her to read and understand the different elements of a narrative, whether it is a story that is told or written. Her **metalanguage** skills, her ability to think about written and oral language and how it is used, will allow her to talk about sounds, letters, words, and sentences, which are required for understanding many elements of literacy.

Dr. Michelle has identified some key components of reading and writing that your child will master over time, all of which have their origins in oral communication. There are lots of different concepts involved in reading, but in this chapter we'll focus on four skills in particular, because they represent the ability to translate oral language skills to the written page. Mastering these skills takes time, but they eventually lead to sharp reading skills.

- **Decoding** refers to mapping the **phoneme**, or speech sound, to the letter (or letter combinations) in order to create a word.
- **Word recognition** is the ability to recognize and read words correctly and effortlessly.
- **Reading comprehension** is the ability to gain information from what is read.
- **Reading fluency** refers to smoothness of reading.

Literacy does not occur by osmosis. When we discussed speech and language development in Chapters 2 and 3, we explained that most typically developing children acquired their skills without much formal instruction. But learning to read and write is different: During their preschool years, kids learn through exposure to books and writing, and when they enter elementary school, by direct instruction regarding letters, sounds, spelling, vocabulary, and storytelling. Your child needs all these skills in order to learn how to read.

Researchers have spent a great deal of time studying why some kids have more success learning to read than others. In 1998, Catherine Snow, an education professor at Harvard University, authored (with input from many other specialists) a book called *Preventing Reading Difficulties in Young Children*. This book was the product of a government-ordered commission on reading, and it identified some of the factors that go into predicting good readers. Snow and other researchers, since the publication of her book, have identified certain predictors of reading success. Among them:

- ○ **Strong early language skills.** A broad vocabulary, mastery of syntax, good receptive language, and listening comprehension have all been shown to contribute to a child's ability to learn to read and/or to superior reading skills when children are older. The ability for a preliterate child to rapidly name pictures of objects also correlates to reading skills. Researchers have determined that this skill is similar to the word recognition skills needed later on in reading.
- ○ **Home environment.** Researchers refer to homes in which books and other written materials are present and used often as **high print homes** or **print-rich environments**. Children who live in such households are exposed to books and other forms of print daily, and these interactions allow them to acquire important preliteracy skills.
- ○ **Socioeconomic status.** Educators, language researchers, and even politicians have determined that there is a literacy gap in the United States. Some language researchers relate this directly to the 30 Million Word Gap (mentioned in Chapter 3), in which it was discovered that parents from lower-income groups tend to talk to their children less frequently than adults from upper-income brackets.

Learning to read and write in English is no picnic. Dr. Michelle and Carlyn both have kids who are learning to read, so they know there are certain characteristics of English that make it particularly tricky for early readers. English is what's referred to as an **alphabetic language**, meaning it uses a set of letters that represent sounds, and these letters are combined to create words. Some English letters correlate to multiple sounds, like the *c* in *city* versus the *c* in *car*. Then you have letters that, when combined, make even different sounds— like *g* combining with *h* in *night*. And sometimes the same letter combinations are pronounced differently, as in *read* (in the present tense, the vowel is a long e, like in *bead*) and *read* (in the past tense, the vowel is a short e, like in *bed*). Take a deep breath! It's hard!

LET'S LOOK AT DEVELOPMENTAL MILESTONES IN LITERACY

Literacy skills unfold in a similar sequence for most typically developing children. But there is a huge variation in when children demonstrate early reading skills, and schools may push reading development at different times; indeed, the introduction of the Common Core curriculum—a set of recognized standards that many states have voluntarily adopted—has, in some places, shifted the expectations as to when children should be meeting certain literacy milestones. And some kids are simply more interested in cracking a book while others want to play with trains, paint, or hop on the jungle gym. As Dr. Michelle explains, **the age ranges for achieving these literacy skills are general; most typically developing children will demonstrate these skills during these age ranges.**

PRELITERACY (PRE-K THROUGH KINDERGARTEN)

Specialists refer to the first stage of reading and writing as **preliteracy,** or **emergent literacy.** Your child will likely learn many of these skills in a preschool or daycare environment or in kindergarten. Children develop them as they are exposed to books, print, and other written materials through a parent or caregiver reading to them. Children in this age range learn best through play, so these reading concepts are best introduced in ways that are fun and that do not seem labor-intensive. **Academic research clearly shows that preliteracy skills are predictive of early reading ability.** Here are some of the emergent literacy skills and principles that your preschooler will likely learn:

○ **Concepts of print.** This refers to the understanding that a letter makes a sound and that letters and sounds can be put together to make a word. Other concepts of print include the knowledge that words make up sentences, and those words and sentences give us information.

○ **Letter knowledge**. This is a two-part ability. One is **letter name knowledge**, which refers to knowing the names of the letters. The other is **letter sound knowledge**, which is the understanding of the sounds that letters and letter combinations make, such as knowing that the letter *s* makes a *ssss* sound and the combination *sh* makes a *shhhh* sound. At first, your child may confuse letters and numbers, but that's perfectly okay.

○ **Book orientation**. This concerns knowing how to hold a book properly (not upside down), knowing to start reading at the beginning of the book, knowing how to turn pages, and knowing that in English we read from left to right and top to bottom.

○ **Phonological awareness**. This refers to the ability to identify and manipulate sounds in words. For kids to develop this skill, they need to be able to really hear and isolate the sounds in words. Some important elements of phonological awareness that your preschool child will likely become familiar with include the ability to:

■ **Identify words in a sentence** by, for example, clapping each time a separate word is heard in that sentence.

■ **Separate syllables in words**, such as by clapping for each syllable in the word *banana*.

■ **Recognize rhyming words**, such as the words *mouse* and *house*, or come up with a word that rhymes with a word when posed with the question, *What rhymes with mouse?*

■ **Separate words into phonemes or speech sounds**, like taking the word *cat* and breaking it into the sounds *c-a-t*.

■ **Blend sounds or syllables to make words**, such as putting *pen-guin* together to make *penguin* or *d-o-g* to make *dog*.

- **Identify and manipulate syllables and sounds in a word,** like replacing the *cup* in *cupcake* with *pan* to make a new word—*pancake*—or taking the *p* out of *pin* and adding a *w* to create *win*.

DR. MICHELLE'S TAKEAWAY

IT'S CRUCIAL FOR your preschooler to master preliteracy concepts. Make learning fun. Read to your child and show him how to read, too.

FROM RESEARCH TO REAL LIFE

ARE MODERN ADVANCES in literacy development more effective? When it comes to electronic books, maybe not. Sure, e-books that can be loaded onto a tablet like an iPad are convenient, and interactive apps that read a book out loud or let a kid play along have entertaining sound effects and graphics. But a growing body of research shows that e-books also may hinder some aspects of early literacy development. For example, psychology researchers at Temple University, including Julia Parish-Morris, studied caregiver interactions with young children as they engaged with traditional books and e-books. She found that, with two types of books, parents used different language with their children. When they used traditional books, they asked questions about the stories, encouraged children to make predictions, and facilitated pre-literacy skills such as page turning and book orientation. But when they used e-books, the parents' language was focused on controlling the book and they spent less time talking about the content of the story. A lot of time was spent pushing buttons and turning the book on and off. Traditional books allow a child to hold the book with the correct orientation and turn the pages—

important prerequisite skills for beginning reading. For young children, traditional books are the best choice.

LEARNING TO READ OR BEGINNING TO READ (KINDERGARTEN THROUGH THIRD GRADE)

Children at this stage of literacy development do not learn their skills simply by being exposed to reading and writing. They need formal instruction. As with language acquisition, reading takes many trials to perfect, and it takes many years to master it. There is also a range as to when schools introduce the concepts of early reading. The advent of the Common Core has in some school districts sped up introduction of these concepts. So one child may learn some of these elements of reading in kindergarten while another may learn the same concepts in second grade. Some of the concepts and skills your child should learn as he begins formal reading instruction include:

○ The **alphabetic principle,** or the concept that words are composed of letters, and those letters represent sounds.

○ **Decoding,** which again means the ability to map the speech sound to letters and letter combinations in order to create a word. Decoding is introduced early on in the reading process and is a key skill needed to become a successful reader. It goes like this: Take the word *kit.* Decoding the word means breaking it up into its separate parts—k + i + t equal *kit.* To do this, your child must have acquired several preliteracy skills. He needs to know each letter and its corresponding sound. He also needs to be able to blend the sounds to create a word. To decode words, he also needs to know certain rules that determine how certain letters or letter combinations sound. If an *e* was added to *kit* to make *kite,* then he must know that the *e* is silent and the vowel becomes a long vowel. The phonological awareness skills that your child practiced in the preliteracy stage, such as blending syllables and sounds to make words, come into play here when he learns how to decode. Becoming a successful decoder takes lots of practice. Some key concepts your child may learn about decoding include:

- **Digraphs**, or two letters that make one sound such as *sh, ch, th, ck,* or *wh.*
- **Multisyllabic words**, or smaller words and syllables within a larger word.
- **Blends**, or consonant clusters of two or three consonants that mesh together to make a distinct sound, such as *bl* in *blue* and *str* in *street.*

○ **Word recognition**, or the ability to quickly recognize words, will also be a skill that children in this age range will be working on. Starting around kindergarten, children begin reading **sight words**, also called **high-frequency words.** These are words that appear commonly in English texts and that children are not supposed to sound out. They must learn to look at them and recognize them holistically, knowing immediately what they mean. Common early sight words include *the, go, what,* or *why.* Children learn sight words through exposure and practice. They also rely on their knowledge of syntax—that important foundation of oral language we discussed in Chapter 3—when reading sight words. When we speak, we use articles like "a," "an," or "the" before a noun. When reading, kids know this rule of English and will expect the sentences they read to follow the same rules as the sentences they say.

○ **Reading comprehension** begins to take hold in this stage. Automatic and quick word recognition allows for comprehension. The strong vocabulary foundation and listening comprehension skills that your child learned as a preschooler will support her comprehension of the texts to which she's introduced. Comprehension improves as decoding is mastered.

Once decoding becomes more automatic, your child should be able to demonstrate a deeper understanding of texts. She should also be developing other linguistic skills that aid her reading comprehension, such as familiarity with different kinds of texts, including understanding the terms "fiction" and "nonfiction" as well as knowing the topic of a text. Children use their general world knowledge to make sense of text and to draw inferences from texts.

○ **Reading fluency** should improve in your child as well. The more opportunities a child is given to practice reading, the more fluency will improve. At this age, reading fluency will encompass not just smoothness of reading, but the ability to read with expression and inflection, with your child's intonation falling at the end of sentences, rising for questions, and becoming more excited for exclamations. As your child's fluency grows, she will begin to master what specialists refer to as **automaticity**—the ability to quickly and accurately read words.

PARENTING TIP

WHEN YOUR CHILD first begins to read, he may read words out loud but have no idea what the text means. Comprehension, decoding, and word recognition don't always develop in parallel. So give him a chance to read the text and then take a turn reading it out loud to him, so he can understand it. Help him figure out what is going on in the text by asking him questions like, *Why did Max go visit the wild things?* His comprehension skills will really grow!

Your child needs all of these fluency, decoding, word recognition, and reading comprehension skills, because once he completes second or third grade, he will move to a new stage of reading, which educators often call the **reading to learn phase**, in which children use reading as a tool to gain critical information. In this phase, children use their established literacy skills to gain more information about a topic they are studying, such as the weather, the solar system, or the Civil War.

DR. MICHELLE'S TAKEAWAY

DECODING, WORD RECOGNITION, and fluency should develop, although not always in parallel. Your child's comprehension should improve so that he can soon begin to read as a way to gain information.

LET'S LOOK AT DEVELOPMENTAL MILESTONES IN WRITING AND SPELLING

Writing goes hand-in-hand with reading. Your preschooler is developing her early writing skills well before she is sitting down to write you a love note. And, as with reading, there is a huge range within which children achieve certain writing milestones. Some preschools and daycares introduce writing skills early; others do not. Some kids show an interest in drawing, a precursor to writing, whereas other kids like to sit on a rug and build with blocks. These differences are okay.

EARLY WRITING (THREE TO FIVE YEARS OLD)

Early writing skills develop before formal writing instruction. Children's early writing skills evolve from scribbling and drawing controlled lines and shapes. Other fine-motor activities—such as painting, stringing beads, and sewing—can help your child practice the dexterity needed for writing. Early writing involves grasping a pencil, crayon, or marker with a child's entire fist and making lines or scribbles. Gradually, through some trial and error and perhaps some instruction from an adult, children will use a **tripod grasp**, using the thumb, index, and middle fingers. Between ages 4 and 6, children master the tripod grasp as well as establish hand dominance, the preference for using either the left or right hand to color, draw, and write.

PARENTING TIP

TEACHING YOUR CHILD to write her name is one of the best ways to practice writing. Encourage your three-year-old to write her name by scribbling some marks. When she gets a little older, practice working on the first letter of her name. Then try having her trace her name. Eventually, you will be able to work with her to mark all sorts of things with her name—from signing birthday cards to labeling her favorite books.

For three-year-olds, writing may consist of lines, circles, semicircles, and, of course, scribbles. Scribbles are great practice for letter writing! *Your child may say I'm writing Happy Birthday!* even if her marks don't resemble actual letters. Give her a high-five. She's showing she's knowledgeable that those marks resemble letters, which make up words, which have meaning.

Between ages 4 and 5, children typically begin to write actual letters that they know. These are usually letters in their name. Some other letters that tend to be easy to write are *T, X,* and *O.* Kids this age typically show they understand that the letters they write are symbols that represent meaning. Kids usually master uppercase letters first and pay no attention to the order of letters or spacing between their letters.

DR. MICHELLE'S TAKEAWAY

ENCOURAGE YOUR CHILD to develop early writing skills, such as scribbling. She will gradually begin to form a few letters.

FORMAL INSTRUCTION (FIVE TO SIX YEARS OLD)

When children enter kindergarten, they are usually given formal instruction in how to correctly write their letters, which is called **letter formation**. Your child will likely be taught to form uppercase and lowercase letters, and as he practices forming these letters, his handwriting will gradually become neater.

Around kindergarten—earlier for some kids, later for others—children are introduced to the concept of spelling. Often, the focus is on writing the letter sounds that the child hears; this is why phonological awareness is so important. Your child may spell just the beginning and ending sounds of a word when she is writing it. She might bring home some schoolwork with some, well, very interestingly spelled words—so interesting that you might have no clue what she means. She may have written *HPE* on a worksheet and you might wonder what she is trying to write. She is probably writing *happy*. Kids often start by writing the sounds that are easiest to hear, focusing on the beginning and end of words. Specialists refer to this as **inventive spelling**, and it is perfectly okay if your kid does a lot of it. **Don't correct her; it's her way of learning how to segment words into sounds and write the letters that correspond with those sounds.**

Children in kindergarten (or so) may also learn how to spell frequently seen words such as "see," "the," "love," and "you." Your child should become familiar with other conventions of print as well, such as spacing between words and writing letters in the order he hears the sounds, in one straight line.

Children usually begin formal instruction in spelling around first grade—although, again, this instruction may begin somewhat earlier for some kids and later for others. They will start to learn that *happy* is actually spelled *h-a-p-p-y*. They will also learn specifically about the **alphabetic rule**—the rule that letter and letter combinations make certain sounds, that words are made up of vowels and consonants, and that you need at least one vowel in each word. Punctuation, spelling rules, and use of capital and lowercase letters may begin to be introduced around this time, too. By the second half of first grade, your child should have perfected capital and lowercase letter formation. In second to third grade, kids continue to practice and perfect these spelling skills, and their writing becomes more lengthy, creative, and self-directed. Your child may be able to write simple stories and can be introduced to various types of writing, such as fiction and nonfiction, how-to books, and persuasive writing.

RED FLAGS
What to Look Out For and When

Because early oral language development is a foundation for literacy, parents and caregivers can sometimes catch signs of reading difficulty before formal instruction of reading begins. At other times, reading issues crop up when formal instruction takes off. This usually occurs around the end of kindergarten or the beginning of first grade. Here are seven key signs of potential reading problems. Some require watchful waiting, and some may trigger a visit to a speech language therapist who specializes in reading or a consultation with a **reading specialist** who has a background in literacy education, usually a graduate degree in reading, and can provide personalized help for your child.

1. Your child was a late talker, or as a toddler was delayed in his language skills. Consult Chapter 3 for the specific milestones, but know that if your child was a late talker as a toddler, and even if his oral language has caught up to his peers by the time he is 4 or 5, he is still at risk for difficulties in learning how to read and write. Research has shown that children with delayed language skills often do not completely master some foundational oral language skills. So check in with a speech language therapist if your child's language continues to lag by age 4, and then make sure you stay in close contact with his teacher when he goes to kindergarten and begins reading.

2. Your child is diagnosed with language impairment. This diagnosis may include a small vocabulary, frequent grammatical errors, or poor listening comprehension. (See Chapter 7 for more information on these types of special concerns.) These oral language skills are necessary for literacy success, so if your child is having difficulty with one or more of them, have him begin or continue to work with a speech language therapist, and be aware that he is likely to need to work with a reading specialist as well.

3. There is a history of reading difficulties in close family members. Reading difficulties tend to run in families, so if a child's parent, sibling, aunt, uncle, or grandparent had problems learning how to read, you'll want to observe carefully how your child is picking up pre-reading and early reading skills. If he seems delayed in any of these skills, monitor your child's literacy development and seek reading help early.

4. Your four- or five-year-old is in a school environment where letters and letter sounds are being taught, and she is having trouble learning them. Some preschools are more academic than others and may teach letters and letter sounds. Some schools may not. But if these concepts have been introduced and your child isn't picking them up, it's time to closely monitor her and seek reading help early.

5. Your child is 6 or older and has difficulty saying multiple speech sounds, such as *th, sh, s, r, l,* **and consonant blends.** Kids with speech sound disorders may be at risk for problems with phonological awareness. You should take him to an evaluation for speech therapy and check in frequently with his teacher about his reading progress, seeking help at the earliest moment.

6. Your child is in kindergarten or first grade and has trouble with phonological awareness skills. Such skills include rhyming, identifying initial sounds, and clapping out syllables. These are important prerequisites for reading and can be predictive of reading success. It is definitely time to check in with a reading specialist and the special education team at your child's school.

7. Your child is in first or second grade and is a slow reader or has difficulty with reading fluency, decoding, or word recognition. It is time to have him evaluated by a reading specialist.

COMMON QUESTIONS,

EXPERT ANSWERS

During her years of being a speech language therapist, Dr. Michelle has heard lots of parents ask her about their children's literacy milestones, because they are so connected to oral language development. Here are some of the most common questions she fields and her answers to them:

QUESTION: *My five-year-old writes some of his letters backward. Is this normal?*

ANSWER: Yes. Practice makes perfect, and it does take time to practice writing letters to get them right. Letter formation—that is, writing uppercase and lowercase letters— is usually introduced in kindergarten and continues to be practiced during the beginning of first grade. Your child should be able to correctly form all his letters by the second half of first grade.

QUESTION: *Are websites or apps good for teaching my child to read?*

ANSWER: Yes and no. Don't rely on a website or app to teach your child to read. You, and your child's teachers, are going to provide that instruction. While not for instructional purposes, some websites or apps are alright to use because they can make tasks like decoding fun. Apps are like ice cream: In moderation, they can be okay. But don't feel like you have to go out and buy something for your child. Your well-worn copy of *Goodnight Moon* is just fine.

QUESTION: *My first-grader is reluctant to read on his own and prefers that I read to him. Should I be concerned?*

ANSWER: Not yet. Most second-graders can engage in independent reading, so don't worry if a child a little younger isn't there yet. He is likely still gaining skills in decoding, fluency, and comprehension. Once those skills seem effortless, he should engage more in independent reading of appropriate books.

QUESTION: *My seven-year-old still has trouble saying her* r *sound. Will this affect her reading?*

ANSWER: No. Kids who have an articulation error with one or two sounds—the common ones are *r* and *s*—are not at particular risk for difficulties with reading. **Kids with multiple speech sound issues may have more difficulty.**

QUESTION: *My kindergartner is having problems learning her letters and numbers but doesn't seem to have any underlying language difficulty. What should I do?*

ANSWER: Start with a vision test. Some kids who have problems learning to read simply need glasses. Check in with your child's regular medical provider, or see if your school provides free vision screenings.

QUESTION: *My child is having problems learning to read. Will he catch up?*

ANSWER: Yes and no. With help (sometimes a lot of help), he will learn to read at grade level. But the research shows that children who struggle to learn to read will always have to work a little harder to achieve the same literacy goals as their peers.

A COMMON CONCERN: DYSLEXIA

Similar to language acquisition, literacy is acquired along a continuum. Some kids catch on quickly and need little instruction to master reading and writing, whereas other kids need a little more help. We'll walk you through ways to get help—both in school and outside of the school setting—in Chapter 8.

A major concern for children who have difficulty learning to read is **dyslexia**, a language-based learning disability having to do with reading. Dyslexia is thought to affect as many as 20 percent of school-age children in the United States. Common indicators include trouble decoding, trouble spelling words, and difficulty with word recognition, fluency, and reading comprehension. Dyslexia runs in families. **Dyslexia is not indicative of delayed cognitive or intellectual skills; children who have dyslexia generally have average or above-average intelligence.**

Children diagnosed with dyslexia take longer to learn to read than their peers, but with help they are able to perform on grade level. The key phrase here is "with help." A large-scale study by researchers at the University of California, Davis and Yale University followed children with dyslexia and typical readers throughout their elementary, middle, and high school years, and their findings indicated that children with dyslexia show disparities in learning as early as first grade. The study's conclusion, published in the *Journal of Pediatrics* in 2015 and written in part by Sally and Bennett Shaywitz, two of the most eminent scholars in the field, was that when it comes to assisting children with dyslexia, the earlier the help comes, the better. Schools often wait until third grade to diagnose dyslexia, but these researchers believe that is just too late. They advocate for earlier screening and intervention.

It will take children with dyslexia longer to learn to read than typically developing children. They will have to practice a lot more, and they will have to work with specialists. This process can take several years. They may struggle in school, because it can be challenging. Children with dyslexia can sometimes develop behavioral issues as well, triggered by their frustration with learning.

Many children with dyslexia also have **dysgraphia**, or difficulty learning to write coherently. Children with dysgraphia usually have sloppy handwriting, do not show appropriate spacing between words, and have difficulty organizing thoughts on paper.

Treatment for dyslexia usually involves teaching kids decoding skills in a systematic way using a multisensory approach—meaning using all their senses, including sight, touch, and hearing—and with a teacher who specializes in reading. A common research-based intervention used with struggling readers is called the **Orton-Gillingham Approach**. Effective treatment strategies involve practice, practice, practice, and more practice with phonological awareness and decoding skills. Don't be surprised if your child with dyslexia has to practice reading a simple word like *dog* many, many times before he can read it on his own.

A PARENT'S PERSPECTIVE

Isaiah's Story

Isaiah was a typically developing preschooler growing up in Brooklyn, New York. He attended a daycare that had an educational component and he thrived. He tested into his local school district's gifted and talented program for kindergarten, but once there, he started to stumble. It took him several months to learn how to write his name, when other kids learned in weeks. He had a hard time learning letters and their sounds. He also began acting out at home and at school. His mom pulled him out of school midyear, and he started kindergarten again the next year at a new school. While that school was a good fit for Isaiah, his reading and writing skills continued to develop differently from his peers. He struggled with phonological awareness. He learned to read, but the process was very, very slow. In third grade, he was diagnosed with developmental dyslexia. In his early elementary years, he switched to various schools; his family struggled to find the perfect fit. During this period of time, Isaiah also developed attention difficulties. Staying interested in school was a huge challenge for him. "When school is hard, you have to have greater motivation to do it," says Isaiah's mom.

Today, Isaiah is thriving in an all-boys high school specializing in kids with learning disabilities. Isaiah's mom's tip: Finding the right school is the key to helping a child with dyslexia. The school needs to have good support for children with specific learning needs, including having teachers trained to help kids with learning difficulties. As a parent, you must advocate for your child to find the best fit.

DR. MICHELLE'S TIPS ON SECRETLY TEACHING YOUR KID TO READ AND WRITE

SHHH . . . DON'T READ this section aloud to your children: Many kids learn to read and write best when it isn't a chore. Here are some of Dr. Michelle's favorite ways to incorporate reading and writing into your child's daily life—without the child even knowing it!

- **Write a message of the day.** When her oldest daughter was learning to read, Dr. Michelle would post a handwritten message in their kitchen every day and invite her daughter to read it. It would begin something like this: *Today is Monday, August 1, and we will go swimming and have a picnic with friends.* Make it fun and simple.

- **Write a question of the day.** Write out a simple question that requires a *yes* or *no* response—for example, *Do you like orange juice?*—and below it create a *yes* column and a *no* column. Have your child write her name in the column that answers the question. This is a great way for your child to practice writing her name, reading questions, and familiarizing herself with the words *yes* and *no*.

- **Have your child help with a recipe.** Your child can read the ingredients and steps and everyone in the family can participate. When Dr. Michelle makes a cake (yes, she uses a box mix), her younger daughter, who is four years old, *reads* the ingredient list with the help of the pictures. Her older daughter, who is seven years old, reads each step aloud from the box.

- **Read street signs out loud.** You'll be amazed at how quickly your child will recognize that the letters S-T-O-P represents the word *stop*. A child who knows the word *no* can find it on many streets signs.
- **Have your child write his birthday and holiday wish lists.** If your child really wants a set of Legos, he might write down the words.

SOME SIMPLE THINGS TO DO AT HOME

Did we mention it's good to read to your children? Early and often. Every day. In the morning, in the afternoon, and in the bath (seriously). Here are Dr. Michelle's tips for raising good readers, as well as Carlyn and Dr. Michelle's favorite books for each age group. There are loads more books, of course—we're just giving you a starter list.

BABIES TO TWO-YEAR-OLDS

It's never too early to introduce a love of reading to your baby. And it's not just about reciting the words on the page. Talk about the books, even if your young audience member does not reply. Get books that have a sensory element—books that are soft or interesting to the touch. Make reading time fun. Here are some other tips:

- Point out words that rhyme.
- Point out a few letters, such as those that begin your child's name.
- Underline each word with your finger as you read.
- Choose books with just a few words on a page. This allows your toddler to understand that the reader is pointing to a particular word while reading.
- Ask your child to point to pictures while you are reading.

Here are a few of our favorite books for this age set:

- *Goodnight Gorilla* by Peggy Rathmann. This unbelievably cute book, with few words, lets young readers identify the words that match the story.
- *From Head to Toe* by Eric Carle. Both of Carlyn's kids loved this book. You get some bonus clapping and gestures from your wee ones.
- *Barnyard Dance* by Sandra Boynton. Pretty much any book by Boynton is a winner at this age, but Dr. Michelle's kids loved this rhyming book.
- *Dear Zoo* by Rod Campbell. This book with flaps is fun for the kiddo and an adult.

PRESCHOOLERS AGES 2 TO 4

Your preschooler is acquiring vital preliteracy skills. In addition to reading to your child, talk to her about the story and encourage her to talk back to you. Here are some other reading tips:

- Ask your child questions about the pictures. Also ask who the characters in the story were, what happened in the story, and what your child thinks will happen next. This will encourage listening comprehension.
- Continue to point out rhyming words and have your child create rhymes. When reading a familiar story together, like *Hop on Pop* by Dr. Seuss, have your child fill in the last word of a phrase or sentence. For example, *We like to hop. We like to hop, we like to hop on top of _____.*
- Point out specific letters, such as those in your child's name.
- Talk about what new vocabulary words mean. If you come across a new word in a book, like *habitat*, explain what it means and give a few examples of different animal habitats.

Some favorite books for this age set include:

○ *Sheep in a Jeep* by Nancy E. Shaw. This is Carlyn's personal favorite. The rhyming is great and the simple story line is fun for little kids (and, occasionally, grown-ups).

○ *Brown Bear, Brown Bear, What Do You See?* by Bill Martin Jr. This book has fun pictures and predictable phrases.

○ *Hop on Pop* by Dr. Seuss. The old master wrote lots of fun and lovable books, but this is an especially great one to introduce as a preliteracy tool because of its easy rhymes.

○ *We Are in a Book!* by Mo Willems. Nothing introduces meta-language better than this book by the wildly popular contemporary children's book author.

○ *The Very Hungry Caterpillar* by Eric Carle. This book is a classic for a reason. Kids have fun turning the pages in this book, and, of course, the story has a magical end.

○ *Chicka Chicka Boom Boom* by Bill Martin Jr. and John Archambault. This book is a fun and colorful way for your child to learn the letters of the alphabet and has catchy rhymes.

KINDERGARTEN TO THIRD GRADE

Keep reading with your child every day. Even if your child has become an independent reader, your job is not done: You should still be reading to him, exposing him to new texts, introducing him to new vocabulary, and showing him that reading is fun! Also, once your child begins formal instruction in reading, encourage him to take a turn reading to you. Here are some tips, from two parents whose children did not always love to read aloud, for getting your child to read aloud to you!

○ Choose books that your child is very familiar with—starting with the ones that you read to her (such as those on our recommended lists). Later, you can move on to newer titles.

○ Get some reading accessories. Carlyn and Dr. Michelle both discovered that their kids were more likely to read when they had some props that make reading fun, such as giant pencils that help highlight words, fun pointers that you can place on your child's finger to help them read along, and book lights that attach to books.

○ Reread stories. Kids love familiarity and repetition, and reading and rereading improves fluency.

○ Practice reading every day. Make it a part of the family routine. At Dr. Michelle's house, everyone reads after dinner, just like everyone brushes their teeth before bedtime. It's just part of the daily routine. You can get creative, such as having your child read to you in the car on the way to school, or to a younger sibling sitting in his high chair.

Here are some books that Dr. Michelle and Carlyn's kids enjoyed reading out loud (and because these kids needed some arm-twisting to read aloud, we know these books are winners!):

○ *Amelia Bedelia* by Peggy Parish. This fun, classic series helps teach kids new vocabulary and the basics of metalanguage.

○ *My Book About Me* by Dr. Seuss. This book gets kids to read *and* write.

○ *The Book with No Pictures* by B. J. Novak. This actor really knows how to get kids to read aloud.

○ *Benny and Penny* by Geoffrey Hayes. This graphic novel series uses thought bubbles, sound effects, and cute characters to tell fun stories. Kids can practice reading with expression and use different voices for each character.

○ *Danny and the Dinosaur* by Syd Hoff. This classic book has been around for ages, and for good reason: It's fun, which makes it motivating to read.

RESOURCES

Here are some of the books and websites that Dr. Michelle likes to turn to provide useful, actionable advice for parents on literacy development.

- The website Reading Rockets, a partnership with public television stations, publishes great articles on everything from motivating your child to read to Common Core literacy standards: *http://www.readingrockets.org/*.
- The Yale Center for Dyslexia and Creativity was established by some of the most respected researchers in the field of dyslexia and serves as a resource for people with dyslexia and their parents and educators: *http://dyslexia.yale.edu/whatisdyslexia.html*.
- *Overcoming Dyslexia*, a book by Sally Shaywitz, one of the leaders of the Yale dyslexia center, chronicles how children grapple with the challenges of dyslexia.
- Read Brightly is a website, connected to the publisher Penguin Random House, that gives lots of tips and suggestions about books for young readers: *http://www.readbrightly.com/*.

6

MORE THAN ONE

A Guide to Bilingualism

MASTERING SPEECH AND LANGUAGE is not easy, as we learned in Chapters 1 through 5. Now try to do it twice over—or more.

Millions of children grow up hearing and speaking more than one language. Mastery of two languages is called **bilingualism**. An important aspect of bilingualism is that someone who is bilingual not only understands a second language, but can speak and read it as well. There are other people who have mastered more than two languages; this is called **multilingualism**. And, of course, there are many of us who can communicate in only one language, which is called **monolingualism**.

Specialists have a range of terminology to refer to the different languages that bilingual children learn. They will often refer to the language that a child was exposed to initially as a child's **first language**; the next language the child learns is called a **second language**. Language specialists also refer to a **heritage language,** or the language that is learned at home, spoken at home, and considered the non-dominant language in the country or region where the speakers live. Twenty percent of people five years of age or over in the United States speak a language other than English in the home, according to

2014 data from the U.S. Census. Spanish is by far the most commonly spoken non-English language, followed by Chinese.

For some families, raising a child with multiple languages is a necessity, because one or both parents will speak a language at home that is different from what the child hears at school. In other instances, a child's parents may not speak another language at home but will go to great lengths to expose their children to a second language—hiring caregivers who speak another language or signing up for a special bilingual preschool or elementary school. Whatever situation may describe your family, there are compelling benefits to bilingualism. Immersion in multiple languages can expose children to new cultures, keep them in touch with their heritage, and prepare them for the globalized world. And there is new evidence that suggests bilingualism helps children become more organized and better problem solvers!

We will be honest: Dr. Michelle's kids speak just one language. So do Carlyn's children (and yes, she does feel very guilty about this, because Carlyn speaks Spanish, having studied and lived abroad during and after college). But we are both in awe of children who are raised with more than one language. Dr. Michelle wholeheartedly supports raising children in a bilingual environment—whether it's with parents who speak their family's heritage language at home, or through a dual-language school, or any other model.

In this chapter, we will focus on the process of how bilingualism, which is increasingly common in the United States, unfolds in childhood development. We will introduce important terminology associated with it, provide some useful tips on how you can raise a bilingual child, explore different models of bilingual education, and point out particular red flags you may face in bilingual child-rearing. Also, for this chapter, Dr. Michelle has turned to the advice of Dr. Nancy Eng—call her Dr. Nancy—a professor at Hunter College who specializes in multilingualism, has a vibrant practice as a speech language therapist to bilingual children, and, best of all, has succeeded in raising bilingual twin daughters!

ARE BABIES BORN TO BE BILINGUAL?

In Chapter 2 we mentioned that when babies are born, they are ready to listen to language. They are **universal perceivers**, meaning that from birth, babies can discriminate and hear differences between speech sounds in the language their parents speak as well as in languages they have never heard before. If your baby hears only English, she will respond differently to sounds that are common in English, such as *p* and *b*, and to sounds that are not used in English, such as the clicks that make up some African languages or the rolled *r* used in Spanish. **The skill of being able to detect differences between any speech sound across languages indicates that babies are capable of learning any language from the time they are born.**

But then something changes. As parents and caregivers begin talking to them more, babies pay attention to the speech sounds in the language or languages they hear frequently, and they become less sensitive to speech sounds that don't occur in those languages. By the time babies are one year old, they no longer heed sounds that are not in their language. Your three-month-old baby was attentive to the clicks he heard in an African language. But by the time your baby is a year old, he would hear the clicks, but he wouldn't pay attention to these sounds anymore, nor ascribe meaning to them the way he would to the English words he hears often. **So the best time to start exposing your baby to a new language is at birth.** He is ready to listen and learn. But don't worry: If you were too busy changing diapers in that first year, it's not too late. Toddlers and young children still have excellent language-acquisition skills and can learn a second language.

DR. MICHELLE'S TAKEAWAY

YOUR INFANT IS listening to you. If you want to raise him bilingually, start early and talk, talk, talk in the language you want him to learn.

LET'S LOOK AT THE MANY FORMS OF BILINGUALISM

Bilingualism comes in different shapes and sizes. A measure of a child's or adult's mastery of a language is called **proficiency,** or the ability to understand, speak, read, and write in a language. A bilingual person can be proficient in both oral and written aspects of a second language or highly proficient in one aspect, such as written language, and less proficient in others, such as oral communication.

In many individuals who are bilingual, one language is considered **dominant,** meaning a person's level of proficiency in that language exceeds their level of proficiency in their other language. Let's say your child's first language was English, but his Spanish-speaking grandparents visited often. He would be likely to speak English with more proficiency than Spanish. Specialists refer to these people as **non-balanced bilinguals.**

The dominant language in non-balanced bilinguals may change depending on how often and with whom the language is spoken and why. For example, a child whose first language was Spanish may become dominant in English after completing kindergarten at an English-speaking school.

When children speak and write in two languages with equal proficiency, specialists refer to them as **balanced bilinguals,** meaning they have acquired all aspects of language equally, including vocabulary, grammar, and complex forms like figurative language. If your child hears a figurative expression in English such as *It's raining cats and dogs*, she knows what it means and, as she grows older, can use the expression herself. In addition, when she hears a figurative expression in Spanish, she also knows what it means and can use it in the appropriate context as well. Balanced bilingualism is considered relatively rare in the United States.

Some people who are exposed to two or more languages are considered to be **semi-proficient** in one or more of them, meaning that their skills in that language are not as developed as their peers.

Semi-proficiency in language may be the result of several situations, such as speaking one language at home and school, and then moving to a new country where a different language is spoken.

With languages, if you don't use them, you lose them. If your child knows two languages, but he suddenly or gradually has less practice listening to and speaking in one of them, then he will demonstrate **attrition,** or language loss. He can lose some or all of his vocabulary and other language skills in that language.

DR. MICHELLE'S TAKEAWAY

BILINGUALISM TAKES MANY forms. The more exposure you give your child the better, because he can lose his language gains.

FROM RESEARCH TO REAL LIFE

DR. ELLEN BIALYSTOK, a psychology professor at York University in Toronto, Canada, has researched the influence of bilingualism on language and cognitive development for more than 35 years, using a variety of methods including behavioral tasks, neuroimaging, and electrophysiology. She has found that bilingual children ages 4 to 8 show superior performance on linguistic and cognitive tasks such as problem solving and maintaining their attention, as compared to children who speak only one language. Her research supports what linguists call the **bilingual advantage**—the idea that people who speak two languages have a leg up on many skills, including both communication and cognitive ones.

Throughout her research, Bialystok has used neuroimaging techniques to find that people who are bilingual use their brains differently; they make cognitive connections in a different way as compared to people who are monolingual, and in some cases these differences provide an advantage to the bilingual speaker. For example, bilingual speakers must attend to one language while inhibiting the other. These opportunities aid in cognitively demanding situations such as multitasking. More recently, Bialystok's research has also been used to show that bilingualism can delay the onset of dementia in older people.

HOW DOES YOUR CHILD BECOME BILINGUAL?

There are numerous ways to expose your child to another language. There is no right or wrong way—and don't let any relatives, teachers, or books tell you differently. But Dr. Michelle does have some tips and background information that can help you figure out the way that may work best for your family.

Cultural attitudes toward bilingualism have changed drastically in the United States in the last several decades, and they will probably continue to shift as long as many different languages are spoken here. There was a time when many immigrant parents actively discouraged bilingualism in this country, often based on concerns that children who learned a heritage language at home would never fully master English. But today, bilingualism tends to be more celebrated in many aspects of American culture—consider all of the Spanish words used on *Sesame Street*.

Linguists and sociologists who study bilingualism have made significant advances to support the concept of the bilingual advantage, showing the positive effects of bilingualism on the brain and in our culture as a whole. More is better!

Are you ready to start at home? **Dr. Michelle believes that as models for their children, parents should speak in the language they are most proficient in and comfortable with.** Typically, this is their first language or heritage language. **Children need to hear appropriate, complete, and grammatically correct language in order**

to learn it best themselves. If parents speak to their children in a language they are not proficient in, they are effectively limiting their child's ability to acquire that language. They may also be limiting the child's ability to acquire a heritage language if the parent decides *not* to speak that language in the home.

DR. NANCY'S PARENTING TIP

LEARNING A LANGUAGE makes the most sense when children see what that language can do for them. So, work hard to establish cultural connections to the language, such as by making regular visits to restaurants where the language is spoken. You can also try language games, such as 20 questions, videos, and storybooks. Make learning a language fun, interesting, and social for your child.

HOW BILINGUAL LANGUAGE ACQUISITION OCCURS

There are two primary ways that multiple language acquisition can occur in young people. **Simultaneous acquisition** occurs when a second language is acquired around the same time as the first language. According to specialists, that means typically sometime before the child is three years old, which is the time in which children's brains are most primed to learn multiple languages. Common examples of simultaneous acquisition include:

- When, in the home, one parent speaks one language and the other parent speaks a different language.
- When a child hears one language at home and a caregiver or nanny speaks another language.

Sequential acquisition occurs when a child learns his first language and then acquires a second language after he turns three years old. As someone who picked up Spanish in elementary school, high school, and college, and then by working and living abroad, Carlyn experienced sequential acquisition. Common examples of sequential acquisition include:

○ When a child is exposed to a first language at home and then acquires a second language when he begins formal schooling, such as entering kindergarten.
○ When a child grows up in one country, learns that country's dominant language, and then moves to another country where a different language is spoken.

Some children who experience either serial acquisition or sequential acquisition of multiple languages never thoroughly learn one of them. This is called an **incomplete acquisition**. It can occur when a child moves from one country to another or begins an education in a new language and then never keeps up with the first language. Sometimes an incomplete acquisition of a language is okay. If your family was in the Netherlands and you come back home, your child might lose his Dutch language skills and you might decide he didn't need his Dutch language anymore because it is so rarely spoken here. **Ultimately, parents need to make sure that their child really is able to master a language if he is to eventually acquire adult language skills.**

THE PATH TO BILINGUAL LANGUAGE DEVELOPMENT

Language specialists refer to a **critical period** for bilingual language acquisition, meaning an important time in early childhood when kids are most primed to learn a new language. Specialists disagree on exactly when the critical period ends: Some say as young as six; others suggest it can last until ten years old. Research has shown that as children get older, it is harder to acquire a second language with ease. This doesn't mean that an adolescent or adult can't acquire another language, but it may become more difficult the older the learner is, and some aspects of the language, such as pronunciation, may be more challenging.

Bilingual children pass through similar speech and language milestones as monolingual children. **No matter how a young child is exposed to different languages, she will follow a similar path to language development as a typically developing child.** She should begin to say first words around her first birthday and be able to combine words into short phrases, such as *Mommy up* or *Want milk* (or the equivalent in another language) by her second birthday.

In Chapter 3, we gave you some milestones for vocabulary development in young children. We noted that kids at 18 months averaged vocabularies of 50 words, and kids around 24 months had an average vocabulary around 300 words. The same milestones apply for children who are learning two languages, but **you can add up the number of words your child has in** *both* **languages to get to that magic number.** But guess what? If your child has a word in one language, it is not likely that he will have the same word in the other language. So, if he says *gato* in Spanish, he will probably not say *cat* in English. Animal sounds and gestures still count as words!

During this time, you may notice your bilingual child going through something called a **silent period.** She will be concentrating on listening and understanding and as a result **may not say any words in her second language.** Parents, caregivers, and specialists usually observe their bilingual children going through a silent period when they are first exposed to a second language. The silent period may last weeks, months, or even up to one year, particularly in toddlers and preschool-age children.

While children under age 3 who learn multiple languages tackle the same milestones as monolingual children, they may have a slightly different way of speaking. Do you remember those four pillars of language that we discussed in Chapter 3—vocabulary, syntax, grammar, and pragmatics? Kids who are learning two languages will develop these elements, too. But they may do some mixing and matching, particularly up until early elementary school. You might notice your child using certain aspects of the syntax rules—such as word order—from one language with the vocabulary of another language. Or she may insert words from one language into sentences from another. This is your child's way of sorting out the different rules for each language. **These patterns are typical and are not cause for concern.**

Bilingual children should pick up the speech sounds in both languages to which they are exposed. It takes monolingual children time to practice and perfect their speech sounds—**and it should take bilingual children roughly the same duration of time to master these speech sounds.** So children who speak both English and Spanish will learn the Spanish rolled r sound and the English r sound, and it will take them about the same amount of tries to perfect these sounds as their peers.

DR. MICHELLE'S TAKEAWAY

EXPECT YOUR BILINGUAL CHILD to meet the same milestones as a monolingual child, but don't be surprised if she goes through a silent period and chooses not to speak one language for a little while.

FROM RESEARCH TO REAL LIFE

CHILDREN WHO ARE adopted from another country can take unique journeys in language acquisition. Many of these children are exposed to the language of their birth-origin country from the day of their birth, and then to a different language once they are adopted and brought to a new country where a new language or languages are used. Many times, little or no exposure to the child's heritage language is maintained. Sharon Glennen, a professor in speech-language pathology at Towson University, specializes in language development of children who are adopted internationally. She has found that children adopted when they are 24 months or younger show huge language growth over the course of the first year that they are introduced to the new language. By that time, they tend to show average performance in their oral language skills. Children who show average language within one year are not at particular risk for literacy delays and usually perform in the average range in school.

Less is known about language and literacy development in children adopted at older ages. Most research suggests that within a year, an internationally adopted child's receptive language skills are close to that of her peers, but the older the child is when she is adopted, the longer it will take her to develop expressive language skills. Older children who have acquired a heritage language will lose that language rapidly—within weeks or months—if they no longer hear that language. The older the child is at the time of adoption, the more difficult it may be for her to acquire a new language, which can negatively affect school performance. If your child is adopted internationally after the early elementary years, be aware of the phenomenon of incomplete language acquisition (discussed earlier in this chapter) and work hard to help her develop all of the language skills in her new language.

BILINGUALISM IN THE SCHOOL SETTING

Bilingualism can be fostered at school as well as in the home.

Dual language schools, in which there are two languages of instruction, are a popular choice for families who speak more than one language as well as for families who want their children to learn another language than the one they speak at home. You can find a dual language program in a nursery school or preschool, as well as in public, private, and charter schools at the elementary, middle, and high school levels. Dual language education has grown rapidly in the United States over the last several decades. There were just a handful of such schools in the 1970s; today there are more than 2,000 nationally, according to the Center for Applied Linguistics, a nonprofit group in Washington, D.C., that advocates for bilingual schooling and helps schools and teachers develop their curriculum. The most popular programs are in Spanish, French, and Chinese (Mandarin).

Different kinds of dual language schools abound. Some schools teach half of their material in one language and half in another. Others may teach 90 percent in one language and 10 percent in another. Schools may also shift the ratio of language instruction as the children grow older.

In some dual language schools, half of the students are English dominant and the other half are dominant in the other language of instruction—say, Spanish. Educators often refer to this arrangement as **two-way immersion.** The main concept behind this model is that both English speakers and the speakers of the other language benefit: The English speakers learn another language and the speakers of the other language learn English. Both groups of children will complete school with proficiency in two languages, achieving what specialists call **biliteracy,** or the ability to read and write in two languages. Every school may operate a bit differently, but often, the language of instruction will alternate each day—instruction in reading, writing, and math will occur in English one day; the next day in the other language. Other schools will switch things up throughout the day. Many of these schools have a specific teacher devoted to English and another teacher to the other language of instruction.

Some schools also use what's called a **total immersion model,** where all instruction takes place in another language. This means that while your child may never have heard a word of French before, he'll step into kindergarten hearing only *oui* rather than *yes*. A nonscientific term for these programs is the sink-or-swim model—your child will either learn the new language or he'll face learning challenges. The idea behind these programs is that in the beginning years of ed-

ucation, children are following simple instructions with a lot of repetition—so it is not a big leap to begin total immersion in another
language. Advocates of these programs point to research that has
shown that kids who went through immersion schooling performed
as well as or better than other learners their age on writing and math
tests. Many of these programs add English instruction in later grades.

Another form of bilingual education for students ages 3–21 is the
system set up for those who do not speak English as their first language. A student whose native language is not English is considered
to be a **limited English proficient student (LEPS),** also referred to
as an **English language learner (ELL).** According to the 2010 Census, Spanish is the dominant language in LEPS students in 46 states.

Some ELL students will receive help from an **English as a second
language (ESL)** teacher or a **teacher of English to speakers of
other languages (TESOL),** who will work with them to develop
proficiency in English, paving the way for them to succeed in an
English-instruction classroom. Schools often follow two models for
children. A teacher who works in the classroom with the child is referred to as an **ESL push-in teacher**, and a teacher who takes the child
out of the classroom for focused lessons is called a **pull-out teacher.**

A PARENT'S PERSPECTIVE

Kaito and Mica's Story

Kaito was born in Tokyo to an English-speaking dad and a Japa-
nese- speaking mom. When he turned 1, he and his parents
moved to the United States, where he continues to live today.
His parents wanted him to still be exposed to the Japanese language and culture. His mom spoke only Japanese to him, he attended Japanese playgroups and preschool, and he heard English
only from his father. As a toddler, Kaito's preferred language was
Japanese. When he was nearly 4, he began attending a pre-K program at a local public school and, within two weeks, English
became his dominant language. He spoke English to his friends

and teachers, and he soon began responding to his mom in English at home.

Mica, Kaito's younger sister, has a slightly different story. Born in the United States, she has always heard English spoken around her. While her mom spoke Japanese to her, she heard a lot of English from her brother Kaito and his friends. So, by the time she turned 2, she had a much broader English vocabulary than Kaito did at that time, including lots of idiomatic expressions, like *Hey!* and *Stop it!*

Kaito and Mica's mom speaks Japanese to both children; if they respond in English, she answers back in Japanese. She also makes Saturdays Japanese-only day in the home, so even the children's English-speaking father keeps up with the language. She tries to explain to Kaito how important the language is to her. She also uses positive motivation to keep her kids connected to Japanese language and culture, like finding fun games, Pokémon cards printed only in Japanese, and comic books and movies in Japanese.

"I believe the best way for them to keep up with the language is to have it come from themselves," says Kaito and Mica's mom.

The whole family also goes on an annual trip to Japan to keep up connections with the language, as well as friends and family. "I think it's important to give them a context to the language," says the children's mom, "such as a Japanese identity based on real connections to its culture and people."

 RED FLAGS
What to Look Out For and When

Bilingual children follow the same language milestones as children who are exposed to one language. In Chapter 3, we identified some red flags for children who are acquiring language skills. **These same red flags apply to children who hear more than one language.** You can flip back to Chapter 3, but as a refresher, we'll again list here some of the most important ones. If you notice these red flags, contact your child's pediatrician or regular medical provider.

○ Your baby does not respond to his name by 12 months.
○ Your baby does not seem to understand familiar language that is directed at her by 12 months.
○ Your baby does not use gestures by 12 months.
○ Your child shows regression in language skills at any age.

Now, here are two red flags specific to children who are acquiring more than one language:

1. Your child experiences a silent period for longer than one year. It is time to contact a speech language therapist specializing in bilingual language development. While bilingual children do proceed through the same developmental milestones as monolingual children, keep in mind that it is common for many multilingual children to experience a silent period in which they continue to hone their receptive language skills but may take a break from speaking words in a new language for weeks or months at a time.

2. Your child is not using words in any language to communicate at age 2. It is time to schedule an evaluation with a speech therapist who specializes in bilingual language development. For monolingual children, we urged you to go to the pediatrician a littler earlier—at about 15 months. However, because we know that the silent period can kick in around then for bilingual children, we suggest that it's okay to wait until your child is two years old.

COMMON QUESTIONS,

EXPERT ANSWERS

While Dr. Michelle does not specialize in bilingualism, she has stayed up to date on current research on bilingualism. And her colleague Dr. Nancy is a speech language therapist who speaks several dialects of Chinese, including Mandarin, Cantonese, and Toisanese, in addition to English. Her clinical practice and academic research focuses on the development and disorders of multilingual acquisition, particularly in children who speak Asian languages. Over the years, both Dr. Michelle and Dr. Nancy have answered hundreds of questions from parents about children's multilingual development. Here are some common questions and their answers.

QUESTION: *My two-year-old is exposed to two languages at home, and he is not saying any words in either language. Does he have a language disorder?*

ANSWER: If your child is not saying any words by age 2, we would suggest checking in with a speech language therapist, especially somebody who specializes in bilingual children. **Typically developing children utter first words at around 12 months of age, regardless of the language to which they are exposed.** This suggests that the onset of first words is not determined by a specific language, but rather by other developmental milestones, like cognitive and neuromotor readiness. Remember that bilingual children may experience a silent period, but a visit to a speech language therapist can help you to understand if your child's language development is on a typical path.

QUESTION: *My bilingual child has a language delay. Should I speak only English to him?*

ANSWER: No. Bilingual children who demonstrate language delays will exhibit the same type of delay, regardless of language. For example, a child who has difficulties using pronouns in one language will also have problems with pronouns in another language. In the case of a bilingual child in a bilingual home, the opportunity to see common characteristics across languages may help a child's language-acquisition experience.

QUESTION: *I'm thinking of raising my child bilingual. Will his language be delayed?*

ANSWER: No! Typically developing children can learn a second language with no difficulties. They follow similar developmental milestones as children learning one language.

QUESTION: *My parents—my child's grandparents—speak only Mandarin to my son, but we don't speak it in the home. Will he learn it?*

ANSWER: Yes. Researchers call this **passive exposure**, and research has shown that it has positive influences on second language acquisition. Young children who grew up overhearing a foreign language without ever having actually learned the language do better when they take that language as a foreign language in college.

QUESTION: *Can my child learn Spanish from watching* Dora the Explorer *on TV?*

ANSWER: No, but there's no need to dis Dora! On the other hand, if you are inclined to have your child watch some TV or videos, then an age-appropriate program in the target language is a good idea. For example, there are American shows and movies that are presented in other languages. Having your child watch the same show more than once can allow him to make sense of what is going on. Watching the same show repeatedly gives a child the satisfaction of mastery.

QUESTION: *I speak to my child in French, but she answers me in English. What should I do?*

ANSWER: Don't give up: Keep speaking to her in French. It is not uncommon to experience resistance from your child. She may want to speak the mainstream language that she hears from her peers, and she may express herself by resisting speaking a heritage language. But keep forging ahead. Your children will thank you later.

A COMMON CONCERN: DELAYED LANGUAGE DEVELOPMENT

The most common concern affecting bilingual children is delayed language development. **When a bilingual child demonstrates a language delay, he will manifest the delay in both languages and display the same issues—such as, say, vocabulary and grammar difficulties—in both languages.** As a result, it will take him longer to learn both languages.

Children who show delayed language in comparison to their peers with no other neurological, social, sensory, or physical contributions are considered to have **language impairment**, a condition that also affects monolingual children and that we'll address in more detail in Chapter 7. Although no studies have specifically examined the incidence of language impairment in bilingual children, it is thought to affect approximately 7 percent of children, which is similar to the incidence in monolingual children. **A bilingual environment does not put a child at risk for language delay.**

— PARENTING TIP —

REMEMBER, ORAL LANGUAGE builds the foundation for reading and writing. Strong oral language skills in both languages are needed to foster literacy. So, don't forget to read to your child in both languages that they are exposed to at home so that they become aware of the sound and letter correspondence rules for each language.

SOME SIMPLE THINGS TO DO AT HOME

It's not easy raising children to be bilingual, and no one knows that better than Dr. Nancy, who herself is raising twin girls in a bilingual environment. When her daughters were young, Dr. Nancy and her husband spoke primarily Mandarin in the home, read books to them in Mandarin, and used Mandarin-speaking babysitters.

Though Dr. Nancy and her husband were diligent in using Mandarin around their children, they couldn't compete with the reality of the schoolyard! The girls wanted to fit in with other kids at their elementary school, so they learned English in a brief time period. By first grade, English was their preferred language: They wanted to speak it all the time. Dr. Nancy knew their choice was inevitable, but the realization that it was happening was disappointing. With determination and focus, she has forged ahead. And so should you.

Here are Dr. Nancy's top tips on raising bilingual children—either by speaking a heritage language at home or by reinforcing a second language that a child may be speaking at school or with another caregiver:

○ Read bilingual books. We can't overemphasize the value of reading to your child, and this applies to raising bilingual children, too. You can choose some of your favorite books from your past or English-language classics translated into another language, like *The Very Hungry Caterpillar* or *Goodnight Moon*.

○ Watch heritage language videos. While we are not big advocates of screen time, an occasional movie night can be a great way to establish a memorable connection to your heritage language.

○ Establish fun connections to your heritage language or the language you want your child to learn by going on outings such as regular dinners or lunches at a Chinese or Latin American restaurant.

○ When everyone needs downtime, choose music played in the heritage language or language you want your child to learn.

○ Participate in playgroups or hire caregivers who speak the heritage language.

○ Continue to speak to your child in her heritage language, even if she responds in English.

○ Sign up for language schools or classes available after school or on weekends. Some of these classes focus on listening and speaking skills, and others are more academic and demand reading and writing as well. Choose the one that is best and most age-appropriate for your child.

○ Take annual trips to a country where the heritage language is spoken. We know, plane tickets are expensive. But if you can save up, consider it an educational and cultural investment.

RESOURCES

Finding good information about raising a bilingual child is not always easy. Websites may take different cultural viewpoints or be short on empirical research. Here are some of Dr. Michelle's favorite research-based resources to check out about bilingual language acquisition and bilingual schooling.

○ The American Speech-Language-Hearing Association (ASHA) has some helpful information on second language acquisition: *http://www.asha.org/public/speech/development/second/*. ASHA has a page on the advantages of being bilingual as well: *http://www.asha.org/public/speech/development/The-Advantages-of-Being-Bilingual/*.

○ If you are concerned about your bilingual child's hearing, speech, or language development, a bilingual professional should be contacted. The Find a Professional page of the ASHA website will help you to find an audiologist or speech language therapist in your geographic area: *http://asha.org/profind/*.

○ The Center for Applied Linguistics (CAL), a nonprofit group based in Washington, D.C., that provides support for bilingual schooling, has resources, research, and news about bilingual education: *http://www.cal.org/*.

○ CAL also has a directory of schools across the United States that provide bilingual education, using many different models of instruction: *http://www.cal.org/resource-center/databases-directories*.

7

SPECIAL CONCERNS
When Things Don't Go as Expected

A S PARENTS OURSELVES, we know that watching your child's development can consume you in ways you never expected. We've said it before and we'll say it again—talking, an essential part of human interaction, is a skill that can take considerable time to master, and sometimes kids have difficulty achieving perfection. For some kids, challenges can last for weeks or months or even years. We know that watching your child confront these challenges can be as tough on a parent as it can be on a child. As a parent and specialist, Dr. Michelle has seen lots of kids grapple with speech and language development, and her goal is to help parents support and inspire their children in this effort.

Doctors, researchers, speech therapists, and educators are still trying to understand just what causes the many difficulties and disorders that kids struggle with, especially when it comes to their abilities to talk and listen. The definitions and labels that researchers and clinicians have come up with assist specialists and parents in identifying problems and prescribing the right treatment. But these labels have limits, too, because our understanding of how communication disorders and difficulties develop and manifest themselves continues to evolve.

There is no singular authority that all doctors, speech language therapists, and educators rely on to define and explain hearing, speech, and language disorders, broadly called **communication disorders**; indeed, specialists don't always agree on the same definition. Speech language therapists and audiologists turn to the American Speech-Language-Hearing Association (ASHA), the national accrediting body of speech-language pathologists and audiologists, for guidance when diagnosing and treating children with these disorders. Another source that clinical experts and researchers frequently turn to is the *Diagnostic and Statistical Manual of Mental Disorders (DSM)*, which is published by the American Psychiatric Association and defines hundreds of disorders affecting children and adults.

In this chapter, we will help you to understand some of the labels and diagnoses you may hear about from specialists. Our discussion will focus on specific difficulties and disorders that have their roots in hearing, speech, and language development, as well as other developmental disorders that can affect these abilities. We will walk you through some of these disorders, point out red flags, and provide resources that will assist you in learning more about these difficulties.

While Dr. Michelle will offer guidance and advice to help you and other caregivers get the most appropriate diagnosis for your child, please keep in mind that only a specialist who has seen your child in person can provide a formal diagnosis.

HEARING DISORDERS: WHEN YOUR CHILD HAS DIFFICULTY DETECTING AND RECOGNIZING SOUNDS

Hearing is foundational for kids' communication. In order to develop language, babies need to hear all the speech sounds in the language or languages to which they are exposed. Individuals with **hearing disorders** have difficulty perceiving sound. Hearing loss can vary from slight or mild (meaning people receive some reduced auditory input) to **deafness** (meaning they receive little to no auditory input).

In Chapter 1, we explained how hearing works in typically developing children and identified the two main types of hearing loss that can occur in kids: **conductive hearing loss**, which is often temporary and can be the result of damage to or fluid in the outer or middle ear, and **sensorineural hearing loss**, which is typically permanent and the result of damage to the hair cells of the inner ear. Children with these types of hearing loss are susceptible to experiencing speech and language delays because they cannot detect all speech sounds in the same way as their peers with normal hearing. If you suspect your child is experiencing hearing problems, if your child is not responding to sound and speech as you would expect, it is time to visit an audiologist to determine if he has a hearing disorder.

AUDITORY PROCESSING DISORDER

Besides hearing loss, there are other auditory difficulties that children can experience. One such difficulty is **auditory processing disorder (APD),** also known as **central auditory processing disorder (CAPD).** APD is a condition that makes it difficult for kids to process auditory information, compromising their ability to understand what other people are saying.

Children with APD have normal hearing abilities—meaning that if they are administered a hearing test, they will hear the beeps at a normal level—but their issues lie in processing, or understanding, spoken language. If, for example, you tell your child, at a normal volume, *Please get a glass of milk from the fridge and bring it carefully into the dining room,* he will be able to hear you. But he may not be able to understand these directions fully or to act on the instructions. Children with APD often have difficulty listening to and following complex directions, especially in a noisy environment like a classroom.

Another challenge for children with APD may be determining where sound is coming from, which is called **localization**. Difficulty listening to and understanding speech, following oral directions, and determining the source of sounds, especially in a noisy classroom environment, can make learning very challenging for children with this disorder.

PARENTING TIP

IT'S IMPORTANT TO get your child's attention first before speaking to him. Achieve eye contact, and then speak slowly and be simple and specific with your language. For example, instead of saying to your child, *Let's get ready to go,* try more specific language, such as *Put your shoes on and get your backpack.* Your child may respond better to this type of direction.

The definition of APD and our understanding of this disorder have evolved in the last several decades, but research in this area is still very much ongoing. Currently, APD is thought to be caused by damage to the auditory pathways in the brain. The auditory message enters the outer ear, travels through the middle and inner ear appropriately, but does not adequately reach the auditory cortex in the brain to be interpreted. Researchers still don't know exactly why this is. Current research studies use **electrophysiological methods**—measuring the brain's response to sound—to understand how the brains of children with APD differ from their typically developing peers. Eventually, this research could lead to more targeted diagnoses and treatments.

A study published in 1997 by Gail Chermak and Frank Musiek, eminent audiology researchers, estimated that APD affects 2 to 3 percent of the pediatric population. Most audiologists tend to diagnose kids with APD when they are at least 7 or 8; it can be tricky to diagnose younger children because many of the current tests used to diagnose the disorder contain tasks and directions that are hard for even typically developing kids to follow. An audiologist will use several tests during an APD evaluation to identify any auditory processing weakness. Your child, in a sound-treated booth, will be asked to perform a variety of tasks, including listening to sounds, syllables, and words and repeating what he has heard. The responses will be used to determine whether your child's processing ability is normal or impaired and, if weaknesses are found, which areas should be targeted during therapy.

This disorder is complicated because so many things contribute to our ability to listen to and understand speech, including attention, memory, and language skills. Children with APD are often also found to have attention deficit disorder, language impairment, and learning disabilities (challenges we are going to discuss later in this chapter). Specialists refer to this as **co-occurrence**. When there are a mix of underlying behavioral and communication issues, it can be really hard to know the specific cause of all of the difficulties. It can be tricky as well to sort out if your child has APD, because its characteristics can look a lot like other disorders, such as attention and behavioral deficits. Dr. Michelle will talk more about treatment options for kids with APD in Chapter 8.

Remember Dr. Mike, Dr. Michelle's audiologist husband whom we met way back in Chapter 1? Here are the five major red flags for APD that Dr. Mike has seen most frequently in children who have already begun elementary school:

RED FLAGS
What to Look Out For and When

1. **Your child has poor listening skills,** especially in the presence of background noise, even at a low level.
2. **Your child consistently has difficulty following complex directions and answering questions.**
3. **Your child frequently misunderstands speech or responds inappropriately to the information he hears.** If this is the case, you should check in with his teacher to see how he listens in class.

4. Your child has difficulty localizing sounds or speech.

5. Your child frequently hears or repeats words incorrectly.

DR. MIKE'S TAKEAWAY

DUE TO THE overlapping of symptoms between APD and other attention, cognition, and speech and language disorders, it is important to have your child evaluated by multiple professionals, including a psychologist, speech language therapist, and an audiologist, to determine the true nature of the disorder.

SPEECH DISORDERS: WHEN YOUR CHILD HAS DIFFICULTY FORMING SPEECH SOUNDS

Speech sounds build the foundation for language. As we discussed in Chapter 2, it takes years for children to accurately produce all speech sounds, and some kids have an easier time than others at mastering the motor movements that turn sounds into words. A baby who is not babbling by 8 months, a 16-month-old who is not saying various speech sounds in her words, or a two-year-old who is intelligible less than half the time are all reasons to check in with a speech language therapist.

Speech disorder is an umbrella term used by specialists to refer to any difficulty in producing speech sounds correctly, consistent difficulty producing speech fluently, or difficulty with phonation (vocal cord vibration) needed to produce speech. We introduced you to one speech disorder, stuttering, in Chapter 4. Another type of speech disorder in children is a **speech sound disorder,** which is a general term for difficulty with the production of speech sounds needed to say words. There are different kinds of speech sound disorders. The most common type is an **articulation disorder**—or the inability to master certain speech sounds at set milestones as we discussed in Chapter 2. (We'll discuss some good treatment options for articulation disorders in Chapter 8.) But there are other, less common, types of speech disorders that can affect kids, too.

STRUCTURALLY BASED SPEECH ISSUES

Sometimes, a speech sound disorder can be the result of a structural difference in a child's mouth. One condition affecting young children is **ankyloglossia**, also known as being **tongue-tied**. This problem occurs when babies are born with a short **lingual frenulum**, a small piece of tissue that connects the underside of your tongue to the floor of your mouth. A short lingual frenulum causes decreased motion of the tongue. Some children born with a tongue-tie do not show any of the common signs of it, such as difficulties nursing, drinking, eating, or making speech sounds. These kids are able to compensate and do not require intervention.

However, in other cases, a child may manifest issues related to a tongue-tie. She may have problems nursing or eating when she is an infant. Or, she may not be able to make speech sounds that require the tongue tip to move up to the top of the mouth, such as the *t* and *d* sounds. In these cases, your child's pediatrician or an ear-nose-throat (ENT) doctor may recommend surgery, likely an outpatient procedure in which the frenulum is snipped.

Dr. Michelle has identified two major red flags for ankyloglossia:

 RED FLAGS
What to Look Out For and When

1. **Your baby experiences persistent difficulty nursing or bottle-feeding.**
2. **Your child who is age 3 or older has difficulty saying all the speech sounds that require a raised tongue tip,** such as *t* and *d*, *n*, *l*, *s*, *z*, and *sh*.

DR. MICHELLE'S TAKEAWAY

IF YOUR INFANT is having trouble nursing or bottle-feeding, or if your three-year-old cannot say the *t, d,* and *n* sounds, consult your pediatrician and/or an ENT to see if it's a tongue-tie.

Two other structural differences in young children that can lead to articulation concerns are a **cleft palate** or a **cleft lip**. A cleft means a gap, so kids with a cleft palate have a gap in the roof of their mouths, while kids with a cleft lip have a gap or split lip. The structural differences caused by cleft lip or cleft palate do not allow the articulators— the tongue, lips, and soft palate to move in the same manner as a child who does not have either of these complications, causing speech sound production difficulties.

Cleft lip or cleft palate develop when babies are in utero, during the first trimester of a mother's pregnancy, when a baby's palate and lips do not form properly. Babies born with a cleft palate have difficulty saying certain speech sounds because their palate has an opening into the nasal cavity. Babies born with a cleft lip can have difficulty saying speech sounds because they may not be able to close their lips together tightly, as when saying sounds such as *p* and *b*, and they may have trouble with sounds that require the lips to be rounded, like *w*.

Today, cleft lip and cleft palate can usually be identified before birth via ultrasound—often during a scan of a baby's full anatomy that takes place around the 20th week of gestation. Both conditions are usually corrected with surgery before the baby's first birthday. According to the U.S. Centers for Disease Control, this condition affects up to 7,000 babies each year in the United States.

Even after receiving surgery, babies with repaired cleft lip and/ or palate may not follow the same developmental speech paths as their peers. This is because babies with clefts had different practice saying speech sounds in babble than typically developing children— and we know that babble is important for building a speech sound repertoire for the words children say. In addition, some children with a repaired cleft palate or lip have difficulties saying certain speech sounds because there may be a buildup of scar tissue on their lips and soft and hard palate, and those parts might not move in the same way as kids who did not have surgery.

Dr. Michelle has identified three specific red flags for infants and children with repaired cleft lip or cleft palate:

 RED FLAGS
What to Look Out For and When

1. **Your infant is not babbling by 8 months.**
2. **Your child has a small repertoire of speech sounds at 12 months.**
3. **Your child doesn't have any words by 16 months.**

DR. MICHELLE'S TAKEAWAY

CHILDREN WITH REPAIRED cleft lip or cleft palate may need speech therapy to help them correctly form speech sounds into words because they may not have had the opportunity to build up a large repertoire of these sounds as babies.

MOTOR SPEECH DISORDERS

Other speech conditions, known as **motor speech disorders**, are the result of difficulty with the motor movements needed to produce speech sounds in words. We mentioned in Chapter 2 that children who have articulation disorders, such as difficulty saying speech sounds such as *r* or *l*, have these speech issues.

Childhood apraxia of speech (CAS), also referred to as **verbal dyspraxia** or simply **apraxia**, is a motor speech disorder where children have difficulty with the motor programming needed to produce speech. When we want to say a word or sentence, our brain develops a plan for our articulators to produce each sound, in the correct order, in a manner that is fluid. Children with CAS have trouble with motor programming, so their brains have difficulty developing the plan for the necessary motor movements to produce speech. Researchers estimate that 0.1 to 0.2 percent of children in the United States have CAS.

Researchers are still trying to figure out how to diagnose CAS properly and distinguish it from other speech and language disorders. Consequently, the number of children who have it is unclear because uniform diagnostic criteria have not been established. However, researchers agree there are three main characteristics of CAS:

1. Inconsistent errors of consonants *and* vowels
2. Difficulty transitioning from one sound to another, meaning that it may take a child longer to move their articulators from one sound to another
3. Inappropriate **prosody**, or rhythm of speech, meaning that the child's intonation may sound a little off or monotone

Children with CAS are difficult to understand because they make many speech sound errors. These errors are inconsistent, which is different from typically developing children who make errors but tend to consistently trip up over the same speech sounds. Sometimes, children with CAS also have difficulty with fine motor skills, such as picking up small objects, and gross motor skills, such as riding a tricycle.

Because apraxia can be hard to distinguish from other speech disorders, Dr. Michelle points out these four specific red flags:

 RED FLAGS
What to Look Out For and When

1. **Your toddler has frequent sensitivity issues with his or her mouth.** A child who has discomfort brushing her teeth may be oversensitive, or a child may be undersensitive, which can be manifest by not feeling objects in her mouth, such as when food remains when eating.

2. **Your child makes inconsistent errors on speech sounds in words.** He may say the same word three different times in three different ways—even a simple word like *cat*.
3. **Your child over age 3 has an age-appropriate vocabulary, but has trouble producing many speech sounds.**
4. **Your child over age 3 is frequently laboring to make a speech sound or say a word.** Specialists call this **groping**.

DR. MICHELLE'S TAKEAWAY

SOMETIMES IT CAN be hard to differentially diagnose apraxia from other severe speech sound disorders. If you think your child demonstrates any of these red flags, contact a speech language therapist; an accurate diagnosis is important to ensure that your child is receiving the most appropriate therapy.

Dysarthria is another motor speech disorder that is characterized by slow, slurred speech. It is caused by damage to the muscles in the face, mouth, and jaw that are needed for articulation, respiration, or phonation, or by damage to the areas of the brain that control speech. This damage, brought on by either weak or paralyzed muscles, results in difficulty producing speech sounds. In children, the main cause of dysarthria is **cerebral palsy**, a neurological disorder that typically occurs from damage sustained to the brain during birth or infancy.

Children with dysarthria have difficulty coordinating their articulation, phonation, or respiration to produce speech. Their speech can be hard to understand because their speech muscles can't move as far, as quickly, or in as coordinated a manner as in typically developing children. Many children with dysarthria have reduced breath support, so they are not able to say as many words per breath. As a consequence, their sentences may be brief.

Because dysarthria is caused by damage to the muscles, it is likely that children may have difficulty with other motor movements such as crawling, walking, and feeding themselves. In addition to delays in babbling, and saying words and sentences, there are three other red flags to watch for:

RED FLAGS
What to Look Out For and When

1. Your child has delayed fine motor milestones, such as difficulty grasping objects like rattles at 6 months and picking up small objects using the thumb and index finger at 9 months.

2. Your child is experiencing delayed gross motor milestones, such as difficulty sitting up without support at 9 months and pulling to stand at 12 months.

3. Your child has difficulty with feeding and eating, such as difficulty nursing or bottle-feeding and eating solid food.

DR. MICHELLE'S TAKEAWAY

IF YOU NOTICE fine and gross motor delays in your baby, consult with your pediatrician, because some motor conditions can cause delays in speech development.

WHAT'S THE DIFFERENCE?

BECAUSE IT CAN be hard to sort through the characteristics of different motor speech issues, parents and caregivers may wonder how to determine what kind of speech disorder their child is experiencing. To illustrate the difference between a child with typical speech development, one with an articulation disorder, one with apraxia, and one with dysarthria, begin by reading the following sentence:

I am very good at riding my bike.

A **typically developing** child should be able to say all the speech sounds in this sentence correctly by the time he's four and a half years old. He may have trouble with the *r* sound, but that's okay at his age.

At the same age, a child with an **articulation disorder** may say the speech sounds in the same sentence like this:

I am bewy dood at widin by bite.

This child is still having trouble with the speech sounds that should be mastered by his age, specifically *v, g, ng,* and *k.* He is also having difficulty with the *r* sound, but at his age this is not cause for concern.

A child with **apraxia,** asked to say this sentence three times, may say it three different ways—showing inconsistent errors on consonants and vowels. His rhythm or prosody when he speaks may also sound unnatural:

I am very dood at widing my yike.
I im bery good at widin my bike.
I am bery dod it riding my kike.

Finally, a four-and-a-half-year-old with **dysarthria** may sound like this:

I dood widin bite.

Reduced breath support is preventing him from saying all the words in the sentence. His errors are similar to the child with an articulation disorder.

LANGUAGE DISORDERS: WHEN YOUR CHILD HAS DIFFICULTY CONVEYING THOUGHTS AND IDEAS THROUGH WORDS

In Chapter 3, we defined language as a symbolic system and explained how it develops in typically developing children. There is a wide span as to when babies and young children start saying their first words and begin putting words together, but the process of language development tends to unfold in an expected pattern in typically developing children. Children learn the building blocks of language as toddlers and practice using the rules of the language they are learning, so by the time they begin kindergarten they have mastered the majority of grammar and syntax rules.

If babies don't respond to their name by 12 months, if toddlers don't have any words by 15 months, and if by age 2 they aren't combining words, they should be checked out by a pediatrician, *and* an evaluation should be sought from a speech language therapist.

Some children do not reach oral language milestones at the same time as their peers and may be labeled as **late talkers**, a condition we discussed in Chapter 3. Late talkers are usually identified when they produce fewer than 50 words and do not combine words into short sentences around their second birthday. Research has shown that late talkers do not ever catch up completely. **Many children who are late talkers show average language skills by the time they enter kindergarten. They are referred to as late bloomers, or recovered late talkers, because they seem to have achieved the language skills of their peers once they begin elementary school. But studies show that these children do not perform as well as their peers in certain language tasks, such as producing complex syntax and morphology forms, and in language-based skills, such as reading and writing.** While many late talkers are later considered late bloomers, it is estimated that about 50 percent of them are later diagnosed with a more severe expression of language delay called **language impairment**, or **language disorder**, which is a persistent difficulty in understanding and/or acquiring spoken and written language.

Keep in mind what we've said about co-occurrence: Language, cognition, learning, attention, and memory all interact with one another. Therefore, **children who have underlying difficulties with processing and producing spoken and written language often experience the co-occurrence of other difficulties, such as attention deficits.** If your child has an underlying attention issue, which we discuss later in this chapter, that can affect her language abilities, too.

LANGUAGE IMPAIRMENT

Some late talkers continue to struggle to acquire language. As preschoolers, these kids have difficulty acquiring new vocabulary and saying sentences and grammar forms, and they are not able to use language effectively to communicate with peers, adults, and teachers. These children are often diagnosed with language impairment, which sometimes may be referred to **as specific language impairment (SLI)** or **primary language impairment (PLI).** Approximately 5 to 7 percent of children in the United States have language impairment. It is usually diagnosed in children who are preschool age—around three or four years old, or when a child enters kindergarten, at around age 5.

Children with language impairment may have difficulty with expressive language or with both receptive and expressive language. Children with language impairment may show language delays in one or more of the different aspects of language, including:

○ **Semantics,** where they may have smaller vocabularies and also may have a hard time finding the word they are looking for, which is called **word-finding difficulty.**
○ **Syntax,** where they may struggle to follow the rules to combine words into sentences.
○ **Morphology,** where they may have difficulty with grammar forms. For example, they may not say the ending of words needed for plurals and possessives (so they would say *the girl cat* instead of *the girl's cat*) and may have frequent difficulty with irregular verbs (such as *he runned* instead of *he ran*) as well as noun-verb agreement (such as *the boy walk to school* instead of *the boy walks to school*).

Language impairment can be diagnosed by a speech language therapist through the administration of a series of language tests, including naming and describing pictures using sentences, saying grammar and sentence forms, following directions, telling stories, and listening to and answering questions. **Children with language impairment have** normal hearing, vision, cognition, sensory, and social skills. While these kids will test normal on an IQ test, they typically have difficulties with verbal memory skills—such as remembering new words. **Language is the primary difficulty in these children**, which is why some researchers refer to this disorder as **primary** or **specific language impairment**. Children with this condition are at particular risk for difficulties learning to read and write, because as we explained in Chapter 5, oral language is the foundation for literacy.

Parents must watch carefully to distinguish between a late bloomer and a child who displays language impairment. Dr. Michelle urges you to look out for these five major red flags for language impairment:

 RED FLAGS
What to Look Out For and When

1. **Your child was a late talker**, had a delayed onset of first words, and did not have words at 16 months.

2. **Your two-year-old struggles to understand language**, such as trouble pointing to body parts and common objects when they are named out loud, or cannot follow simple commands such as *Stand up*.

3. **Your two-and-a-half-year-old has difficulty using language to express daily needs and wants.** Most kids this age should be able to express their everyday needs through words.

4. **Your three-year-old never went through a word spurt**—a rapid growth in vocabulary over the course of several months.

5. **Your three-year-old doesn't say sentences and grammar forms.** Three-year-olds do not say all grammar forms correctly, but they should be using words to form sentences with three or four words that contain pronouns and articles, and they should be able to use the plural, past tense, and possessive forms.

DR. MICHELLE'S TAKEAWAY

IF YOUR CHILD is a late talker, meaning she had fewer than 50 words at 24 months, consult with your pediatrician and schedule an evaluation with a speech language therapist, even if you think she has recovered. She could be at risk for language impairment.

WHAT'S THE DIFFERENCE?

IT'S HARD TO know if a two-year-old who is a late talker is going to turn out to be a late bloomer—a child who basically recovers from her delayed onset of oral language—or if she will go on to be diagnosed with a language impairment as a preschooler. Studies by researchers such as Leslie Rescorla and Rhea Paul, who have followed late talkers over several years, have identified some important factors that may suggest which path a child may follow. Toddlers who show the following characteristics are likely to be late bloomers and will more or less recover from their delay:

- **They consistently use strategies other than oral language** to communicate their needs, such as using gestures and pointing and shaking their head yes or no.
- **They do not show delays in receptive language—** the ability to understand spoken language—but do show delays in expressive language.

Toddlers who show the following characteristics are likely to be diagnosed with language impairment:

- They show delays in both expressive and receptive language.
- They have a limited speech sound repertoire.
- They show few compensatory strategies to communicate, such as using gestures or shaking their head yes or no to communicate their wants.
- They have a close family member, such as a parent or sibling, who had language impairment as a child.

SOCIAL COMMUNICATION DISORDER

Some children have a disorder that affects primarily **pragmatic language**, or the way they use language appropriately in social situations. This diagnostic category, called **social (pragmatic) communication disorder**, was added to the fifth edition of the *Diagnostic and Statistical Manual of Mental Disorders (DSM-5)*, released in 2013, so many clinical specialists are still working on how to diagnose children with it in their practices. Children with social communication disorder have trouble with the pragmatic aspects of language—with its social rules and conventions—leading to problems in social situations. For example:

- They have difficulty taking turns when talking.
- They have difficulty staying on topic.
- They have difficulty varying the way they speak, such as understanding what language to use with peers, teachers, family members, and other adults.
- They have difficulty understanding nonverbal cues or body language, such as facial expressions.
- They have difficulty maintaining appropriate eye contact. Children with social communication disorder often show fleeting eye contact.

In addition, children with social communication disorder may have other co-occurring conditions, including language impairment or attention deficit disorder.

Because social communication disorder was only recently added to the *DSM*, Dr. Michelle and other clinicians are still identifying its most common red flags. However, here are four red flags for social communication issues:

 RED FLAGS
What to Look Out For and When

1. Your two-year-old has difficulty with greetings. Even if you have a shy child, by this age he should be able to give a wave or say a quick hello or good-bye to peers or adults when he is in a familiar environment.

2. Your three-year-old does not respond appropriately to simple questions. You may say something to your child like, *What do you want for breakfast?* If he has social communication disorder, he might consistently respond by veering off topic.

3. Your four-year-old does not consistently maintain the conversation topic with peers or adults for two or more turns. Rather than participating in the give-and-take of conversation, your child may change topics completely or he may consistently try to dominate the conversation, not giving others a chance to talk.

4. Your six-year-old has trouble grasping figurative language, or language that means something other than its literal definition. Kids with social communication disorders may have issues understanding even simple figurative expressions such as, *I'm dying of hunger!*

DR. MICHELLE'S TAKEAWAY

IF YOU NOTICE your child has difficulty communicating in a range of social settings, check in with your child's pediatrician and seek an evaluation from a speech language therapist. Your pediatrician may also recommend a visit to a developmental psychologist.

FROM RESEARCH TO REAL LIFE

CHILDREN WHO HAD underlying language (or speech *and* language) difficulties as toddlers or preschoolers are often diagnosed with a **learning disability (LD)** when they are in elementary school. A learning disability, also called a **specific learning disorder**, is an umbrella term that refers to difficulty mastering specific areas of learning.

Many times, the term **language-based learning disabilities** is used to refer to difficulties with reading, spelling, and writing. Two common learning disabilities (which we first mentioned in Chapter 5) are **dyslexia**, the difficulty with reading, and **dysgraphia**, the difficulty with writing. Learning disabilities are characterized as being persistent—that is, even with intervention or extra help, kids will not catch up and will continue to have problems with particular aspects of learning. And while learning disabilities affect a specific academic area, they cannot be viewed in isolation: Certain learning skills influence the ability to acquire other ones. **Literacy skills are essential to be successful in any academic subject, including math, social studies, science, or language arts.**

A 2014 article, "Language Disorders *Are* Learning Disabilities," published in the journal *Topics in Language Disorders* by professors in speech-language pathology Lei Sun and Geraldine Wallach, suggests a strong relationship between early language disorders and school-age learning disorders.

The authors suggest that **many children diagnosed with learning disabilities in elementary school have an underlying language disorder whose primary manifestations have changed over time.** Often, children who were diagnosed with language impairment in preschool later receive a new diagnosis in elementary school: learning disability. These children do not have a new disorder, the researchers suggest, but rather the academic demands of a third-grader—such as reading comprehension of complex texts—are different from the academic demands of a preschooler—such as learning the alphabet—so the child's underlying deficit in language is simply manifest differently. In their article the professors urge—as Dr. Michelle does, too—that parents, teachers, and speech language therapists work together to help children address their learning challenges. And it can be done! In Chapter 8, we will help you find ways to get great help for your child.

OTHER DISORDERS THAT AFFECT YOUR CHILD'S ABILITY TO COMMUNICATE

Sometimes kids have difficulty with hearing, speech, or language development that is secondary to a particular neurodevelopmental disorder. That means that an underlying neurodevelopmental issue exists, and your child's speech and language is affected *because* of it. **Neurodevelopmental disorders** are conditions that occur before birth or early in childhood that negatively affect social, academic, communication, or daily living functioning.

ATTENTION DEFICIT (WITH HYPERACTIVITY) DISORDER

Children with **attention deficit disorder (ADD)** have difficulty maintaining attention to tasks, and their inattention interferes with social development and academic functioning. Children who show hyperactivity in addition to inattention have **attention deficit hyperactivity disorder (ADHD).** ADHD is found in about 5 percent of school-age children in the United States. The following five red flags may indicate that your child has ADD/ADHD:

 RED FLAGS
What to Look Out For and When

1. You child has **difficulties sustaining attention** to complete play-based activities and schoolwork.
2. **Your child has trouble organizing materials,** including the inability to follow through with activities or schoolwork.
3. **Your child doesn't seem to listen when spoken to.**
4. **Your child is easily distracted by background noise.**
5. **Your child is forgetful in his daily routines.**

ADD/ADHD does not cause speech and language delays, but these conditions often co-occur in children with attention difficulties. And because the ability to listen to and pay attention to words, understand instructions, organize materials, and work in the presence of distractions is necessary for speech, language, and literacy development, and certainly assists in academic success, children with attention deficits are at risk for learning disabilities.

DR. MICHELLE'S TAKEAWAY

IF YOUR CHILD has an attention deficit, then following instructions, listening in class, and keeping up with everyday conversation may be hard. When speaking with your child, keep focused on one topic at a time and reduce interruptions.

FROM RESEARCH TO REAL LIFE

DR. MICHELLE'S SCHOLARLY research has focused on understanding *why* some toddlers have a late start to talking and what role attention plays. In a 2015 study published in the *Journal of Child Language,* she found that late talkers show differences in attention allocation as compared to their typically developing peers. When engaged in a task centered on learning a new word, toddlers who are late talkers did not look at or manipulate new objects for the same duration as toddlers with larger vocabularies. It is possible that delays in attention allocation contribute to the early language delay in toddlers identified as late talkers. **Give toddlers who are late talkers more time to manipulate and explore new objects.** They also should hear the names and definitions of objects *lots* of times in order to facilitate learning new words.

AUTISM SPECTRUM DISORDER

Autism spectrum disorder (ASD) is a neurodevelopmental childhood disorder that can be identified by two main characteristics. The first characteristic is that children have challenges with social communication and social interaction. Listening to and responding to language is difficult. Children with ASD also have trouble engaging in verbal communication to express their needs. **Echolalia,** or repeating (echoing) words, phrases, or sentences that are said to them, occurs frequently in these children as well.

The second characteristic of children with ASD is restricted, repetitive patterns of behavior or activities. Young children enjoy repetition—you can probably recite your child's favorite books because you have read them so many times—but children with ASD engage in repetitive behavior that is *very* restricted. For instance, they will play with only one toy, such as a red car, to the exclusion of all other toys, and they may engage in turning the wheels repeatedly.

Often, the first sign of autism is slow expressive language development. However, signs of ASD related to early social communication can be observed even before children should be saying words. Five specific red flags for ASD that are manifested in kids' earliest communication include:

 RED FLAGS
What to Look Out For and When

1. **Your baby doesn't smile** in response to social interaction by 6 months.
2. **Your baby doesn't engage in back-and-forth turn taking** with smiles or sounds by 9 months.
3. **Your baby does not use any gestures,** like waving her hands for hi and bye, or pointing or shaking her head yes and no, by 12 months.
4. **Your baby does not respond when you call his name** by 12 months.
5. **Your baby loses speech or language at any age.** Some children diagnosed with ASD show a period of typical development, then show signs of regression.

DR. MICHELLE'S TAKEAWAY

TYPICALLY DEVELOPING BABIES show signs of social communication before they can say words. In babies with autism, early social communication is delayed. This certainly warrants a check-in with your pediatrician.

SELECTIVE MUTISM

Another condition that can negatively affect a child's ability to communicate is **selective mutism.** Children who have this disorder use speech and language to communicate appropriately in some social settings, such as at home, but do not use speech and language to communicate in other social settings, such as at school. Sure, many children may take time to warm up and become comfortable during the first month of a transition, like a move to a new school, but kids with selective mutism never break through. It can affect social interactions with peers, and it may also affect academic skills such as word recognition, reading fluency, and narrative skills.

Children with selective mutism are able to communicate verbally, and their language skills are likely age-appropriate, but extreme shyness or anxiety prevents them from speaking in certain situations. The condition is currently classified by the *DSM* as an **anxiety disorder**, meaning it has its roots in an underlying psychological state, rather than in language development or cognition.

Sometimes it is hard to know if a child is very shy or showing signs of selective mutism. Two red flags for selective mutism are that:

 RED FLAGS
What to Look Out For and When

1. Your child who is age 3 or older shows a refusal to speak in certain situations, persisting longer than two months. Some children need time to warm up and become comfortable with adults and peers in a new environment. But after a few weeks, even very shy children will adjust to their new routine.

2. Your child's refusal to speak is interfering with social or academic functioning. A child who refuses to tell the teacher when he has to go to the bathroom or who does not respond to a peer who is trying to initiate play may encounter social difficulties in school.

DR. MICHELLE'S TAKEAWAY

BECAUSE SELECTIVE MUTISM is considered an anxiety disorder, a psychologist or other mental health professional would evaluate and diagnose this condition. If you think your child may be exhibiting signs of selective mutism, you might also want to consult a speech language therapist to determine if the child's language skills, when she uses them, are age appropriate.

RESOURCES

Sorting through all the online information that you may find on different types of communication disorders can be overwhelming. Dr. Michelle always looks to medically and scientifically sound sites. Here are some websites she recommends to help you get more information about the specific conditions discussed in this chapter.

○ For a detailed overview on APD, check out the American Speech-Language-Hearing Association (ASHA): *http://www. asha.org/public/hearing/Understanding-Auditory-Processing-Disorders-in-Children/.*

○ The American Academy of Otolaryngology—Head and Neck Surgery provides helpful medical information about tongue-tie, including the surgery involved: *http://www.entnet.org/ content/tongue-tie-ankyloglossia.*

○ The Centers for Disease Control provides facts about cleft lip and palate: *http://www.cdc.gov/ncbddd/birthdefects/cleftlip. html.*

   • ASHA also has a helpful section about cleft lip and palate and their implications for speech development: *http://www.asha.org/public/speech/disorders/CleftLip/.*

○ The National Institutes of Health (NIH) has a web page about apraxia that notes the mystery of its causes: *https://www.nidcd.nih.gov/health/apraxia-speech.*

- The NIH provides a medically sound resource on language impairment, including identifying some important new research on its possible causes: *https://www.nidcd.nih.gov/health/specific-language-impairment.*

○ The American Psychiatric Association, which publishes the *DSM*, has a fact sheet about the relatively new diagnostic category of social communication disorder: *http://www.dsm5.org/Documents/Social%20Communication%20Disorder%20Fact%20Sheet.pdf.*

○ The National Institute of Mental Health provides information about attention deficits: *http://www.nimh.nih.gov/health/publications/attention-deficit-hyperactivity-disorder-easy-to-read/index.shtml.*

○ Autism Speaks is an organization that provides resources for families with ASD and funding for research: *https://www.autismspeaks.org/.*

○ The Child Mind Institute, an advocacy group for children with a wide range of mental health issues, provides facts and questions and answers about selective mutism: *http://childmind.org/topics/disorders/selective-mutism/.*

8

GETTING HELP

Who to See, Where to Go, and What Your Therapy Options Are

FOR SOME CHILDREN, listening and talking comes easily. But other kids need help hitting the important milestones. It can be hard to know just what difficulties your child is having, but in the end, you know your child best.

Navigating the different channels to get that help is a lot like parenting in general: It takes equal doses of knowledge, patience, love, and grit. Getting help can be a complicated process, as there are many factors involved. Making sure your child not only gets that help, but *gets the right kind of help*, can really be the equivalent of a parenting endurance test. But if you have a concern about any aspect of your child's development—hearing, speech, language, feeding, motor skills, cognition, or social skills—then you need to contact a specialist in that area.

In this chapter, we will tell you who to see for the therapy your child needs, where to go to get that treatment, and what kinds of speech language therapy your child may receive. We will also give you some basic information on the laws that regulate the provision of therapies for young children and Dr. Michelle's tried-and-true tips on seeking help—everything from what to talk about in an evaluation to what to expect from speech and language therapy sessions.

If your child does need help, know that you are not alone. In 2013, the most common reason that preschool children ages 3 to 5 got state and federally funded extra help was for speech and language delays, according to a 2015 U.S. Department of Education report to Congress on the implementation of the Individuals with Disabilities Education Act.

GETTING STARTED ON GETTING HELP

The initial step in getting help for your child is a called an **assessment** or **evaluation**, which refers to the process of gathering information from you, your child, and possibly your child's teachers about his communication abilities and difficulties.

During the evaluation, a speech language therapist will speak with you to learn about your child's medical, developmental, and family history. If your child attends daycare, preschool, or elementary school, the therapist may also observe him in his interactions with peers and teachers. Your child's speech, language, and communication skills will also be evaluated through both informal activities, such as playing, as well as formal tests. The tests may require skills such as naming pictures, pointing to pictures, answering questions, saying words and sentences, and telling stories. The results of the tests will be indicated by a score that represents how the child is performing in those areas as compared to typically developing peers of the same age. The therapist will determine if it is appropriate for your child to receive therapy based on a combination of the scores on these tests, as well as the evaluator's impressions and, possibly, your concerns. Usually, your child's score is the salient factor.

The speech language therapist will interpret the information that is gathered during the assessment to make a decision about the presence or absence of a communication disorder, and if one exists, she will provide a **diagnosis**, or a description of the communication disorder. Speech language therapists can diagnose a range of communication disorders, including articulation disorder, a fluency disorder (typically, stuttering), expressive and/or receptive language disorder, and a pragmatic language disorder. **An appropriate diagnosis is important because it is usually required to get health insurance coverage for the condition or to qualify for special education services in schools.**

If a diagnosis is established, the speech language therapist will then recommend **speech language therapy** (which can also be referred to as **intervention**), which entails focused lessons on improving communication. She will also provide a **prognosis**, or a prediction of how well the child will improve with therapy. The diagnosis and the characteristics of the child and the family will determine the type of therapy that is most appropriate for each child. We'll tell you more about some different types of speech and language therapy later in this chapter.

Getting help is so important for your child's development. We know that there is variation in how children's talking skills unfold, but kids who have delays—whether those are small delays or big delays—can only be aided by extra help. Pursuing speech language therapy for a child who shows delays is important because oral language builds the foundation for academic success in elementary school. A speech language therapist will also work with your child and your family to improve communication, which should decrease frustration for everyone and can aid your child in social settings, too. But speech language therapy is not always a cure, and in many cases it may last months or even years; talking and listening take a lot of practice for some kids. Developmental skills build on each other, so it's important to begin therapy as soon as a delay is detected.

Assessment and intervention come in all different shapes and sizes. They can be free, expensive, or somewhere in between. Evaluation and therapy can take place in the home, at school, or at the office of a professional. In the sections that follow, we'll explain everything you need to know about *who* you will visit to get help and *how* to get different services for your child.

DR. MICHELLE'S GUIDE TO
AN EVALUATION

Dr. Michelle has evaluated hundreds of kids and coached lots of parents through the process of having their child evaluated. Here are some of her tips about how to prepare for a speech and language evaluation:

- **Be prepared to explain how your child's communication difficulties affect his everyday life,** including at home and at school and when communicating with family, friends, peers, and teachers.
- **Be ready to give specific examples of these communication difficulties.** Try doing a short video recording at home or school or on the playground to show the evaluator an example of your child's communication issues, or write down specific instances of issues your child faces. The speech language therapist who evaluates your child may rely heavily on a parent, caregiver, and teacher report and might observe and interact with your child for only an hour or two.
- **Try to be present for all of the evaluation** if you can. This will allow you to observe your child and report to the evaluator if the concerning behaviors were displayed during the evaluation. Keep in mind that for school-age kids, the evaluation may take place in the school setting and you may not be present for it, although you will likely be interviewed about your child's birth and developmental history as well as speech and language milestones and current communication.
- **Familiarize yourself with some terminology.** Knowing some general terms about speech and

language development, like pragmatics, syntax, and articulation, as well as some terms about the difficulties your child may be experiencing, like apraxia, dysarthria, or auditory processing disorder, can be helpful. A good place to look? This book!

MEET THE PROFESSIONALS

A big cast of characters is available both to help you and your child find out what help she needs and to provide the needed services. Keep in mind that it's very likely your child will need to see more than one specialist to gain a complete understanding of her underlying challenges. As you may remember from Chapter 7, many developmental difficulties co-occur with each other. This means it can often take several tries to determine the reason your child is experiencing a communication disorder, and it's common if your child receives multiple, overlapping diagnoses such as attention deficit disorder with hyperactivity (ADHD) *and* expressive language disorder. What follows are some professionals whom your child may see to receive therapy and/or to help you decide if your child needs a particular type of therapy.

SPEECH-LANGUAGE PATHOLOGIST

A **speech-language pathologist** is a **communication specialist** who may also be referred to as a **speech language therapist** or simply a **speech therapist.** This individual will have a graduate degree in communication sciences and disorders. A speech-language pathologist must have a state license to practice; the majority also hold a Certificate of Clinical Competence (CCC) issued by the American Speech-Language-Hearing Association (ASHA). A speech language therapist can help your child with challenges related to speech, language, reading, listening, and social interaction skills. Many speech-language pathologists specialize in working with children with particular issues or disorders. For example, some speech language therapists specialize in hearing disorders, others in stuttering or reading difficulties.

AUDIOLOGIST

An **audiologist** is a **hearing specialist**. A professional in this field will have an advanced degree in audiology (either a master's or doctoral degree) and hold a license in the state where they practice; the majority hold an ASHA CCC certification. You would take your child to an audiologist to evaluate a hearing disorder or deficit and provide amplification (hearing aids and other technology). Some audiologists specialize in testing babies, children, or children with special needs. Also, audiologists can evaluate balance disorders.

EAR-NOSE-THROAT PHYSICIAN

An **ear-nose-throat (ENT)** doctor, or **otolaryngologist,** is a medical doctor who specializes in the aforementioned areas of the body. Some ENTs specialize in pediatrics. ENTs can prescribe medication and perform surgeries (such as placing tubes in the ear or removing tonsils and adenoids). You should take your child to an ENT if you suspect he has a hearing disorder or hearing loss. Audiologists work with ENTs to identify and treat hearing and balance disorders.

OCCUPATIONAL THERAPIST

An **occupational therapist (OT)** helps people improve skills needed to function in everyday activities. For kids, this means helping them with skills needed to participate at home, in school, and during social interactions, such as how to play with and manipulate toys, how to hold a pencil to form letters correctly, and how to feed and dress themselves independently.

FEEDING SPECIALIST

A **feeding specialist** helps babies or toddlers with the motor skills required for eating, such as chewing and swallowing. Remember, some kids who have speech issues also experience difficulties in eating, because both have their roots in oral motor skills. Both speech language therapists and occupational therapists can be feeding specialists.

DEVELOPMENTAL PSYCHOLOGIST/ EDUCATIONAL PSYCHOLOGIST

A **developmental psychologist** or **educational psychologist** can help children who are having difficulty in school related to social, emotional, or academic problems. Psychologists diagnose conditions such as autism, dyslexia, and dysgraphia, and they work with speech language therapists when providing treatment for these conditions.

SPECIALIZED TEACHER

A **specialized teacher** is one who can help your child with a specific learning issue, such as a learning disability or reading delay. There are different types of specialized teachers:

- ○ A **special education teacher** specializes in teaching kids who have learning difficulties. A special education teacher can work in classrooms where all students have special learning needs; can collaborate with a general education teacher; or can travel from class to class or school to school to work individually with children in general education settings who are having difficulty with certain aspects of learning.
- ○ A **reading specialist** helps children who are struggling with reading and writing skills. This specialist most frequently

works with children in small groups but may also work with the classroom teacher and lead classroom literacy lessons.

○ A **teacher of the deaf and hard of hearing** works with children who are hearing impaired or those who partially or completely lack the sense of hearing. Today, most children who have hearing impairment are in general education classrooms. This specialized teacher works alongside classroom teachers to provide extra support to students with hearing loss.

○ An **English as a second language (ESL)** teacher, sometimes called a **teacher of English to speakers of other languages (TESOL),** helps children whose first language is not English learn to read, write, and communicate in order to be successful in social and academic settings.

PUBLIC OPTIONS FOR GETTING HELP FOR YOUR CHILD

There are a number of routes you can take to get therapy for your child. Some are public, meaning that they are free or low-cost and available to all who qualify. Other routes are private, meaning that you will pay for therapy for your child, either out of your own pocket, through your insurance coverage, or a combination. **There is no right answer about which option is best for you and your child.** Some parents choose to look first at publicly funded options. Others go right into the paying options, perhaps because they already know a great speech language therapist they want to work with or they simply don't want to tackle the bureaucracy of a public system. And some parents do both—they get free services *and* they supplement them with services they pay for on their own. Some start right away with paying for therapy themselves while they go through the sometimes-arduous processes of seeking free services.

First, we are going to tell you about the publicly funded options to get help for your child. Then Dr. Michelle will tell you about various other private ways that you can receive therapy for your child—including some ways that may not burn a hole in your pocket.

A little background: The landscape for the way free services and interventions are provided for young children in the United States has been shaped by federal law. It's a good thing, because Carlyn is a former legal reporter, and she enjoys telling you about how laws work.

The main U.S. law you need to know about is called the **Individuals with Disabilities in Education Act, or the IDEA,** which was passed in 1990 and has been updated several times. The idea (get it?) behind the IDEA is that **children with disabilities (and that's the word the law uses, although it's not our favorite) get a free and appropriate public education. Every child in the United States—who meets the criteria—is entitled to free services.**

Each state implements the IDEA on its own. Each state has its own eligibility requirements, has its own standards, and provides its own services. **So, while there is a federal mandate to provide free services to kids in need, there's a lot of variation in how different services are actually given out**. There is also a lot of variation by state as to who qualifies for different services—what specialists refer to as **eligibility**. In addition, some states have their own laws and regulations that cover additional services, which means that your options for your child might be different from your cousin's in another state.

Have the politicians who have passed these laws and the regulators and educators who have implemented them gotten everything completely right? No. (If they did, we probably wouldn't need to write this chapter!) But this is the system we have now, and in many areas and for many children and their families it works.

In the sections that follow, Dr. Michelle discusses the different systems available to obtain free (or, in some cases, mostly free) services. Please keep in mind that there's a lot of variation in the provision of these services depending on where you live and whether you have an infant or a school-age child.

EARLY INTERVENTION SERVICES (BIRTH TO AGE 3)

According to the IDEA, every state must have a program to provide therapies to kids with developmental delays from birth to three years. These programs are usually called **Early Intervention (EI)** or simply **Birth to 3**. In many states, these services are free; in some states, they are publicly funded, but you may be asked to pay for a portion of certain services on a sliding-scale basis.

If your baby was born with a hearing loss, the doctors at the hospital may refer you to your local EI program so that she can start receiving services right away. Or, let's say your little one is 16 months old and you notice she's not saying any words yet (refer to Chapter 3, for Dr. Michelle's guidelines on when kids acquire their first words), then you might want to start your search for a speech and language evaluation by calling your state, city, or county's Early Intervention program to seek help. (Because every place has a different program, you're probably going to have to do an online search for the phone number.)

Your child's pediatrician or teacher could also refer your child to the state's Early Intervention program. **Under part of the IDEA called Child Find, states are required to refer kids who they think might need extra help to get evaluated for services.** You need to give consent for your child to be evaluated or receive services.

Your child will receive an evaluation to determine if he's eligible for services. Specialists in early childhood development will look at *all* aspects of your child's development during the evaluation, rather than just the aspects that you, a teacher, or a medical professional may be concerned about. Then, they'll determine whether your child qualifies for Early Intervention services. **The threshold for whether your child qualifies for these services depends on what state you reside in.** (Go to the Resources section at the end of this chapter for more information about how to look up your state's criteria.) Most states use a formula to determine eligibility. For example, some states grant services if a child is deemed to be 25 percent delayed from a typically developing child; others will grant services if a child is determined to be 50 percent delayed.

PARENTING TIP

DR. MICHELLE HAS witnessed hundreds of parents go through this process, and she knows that it can be stressful. **If your child doesn't get free services, it doesn't mean he doesn't have a delay or difficulty.** Look for other options for therapy—keep reading this chapter!

If your child qualifies for services, you'll receive an **Individual Family Service Plan,** or **IFSP**, which is a legal document that spells out the services your child is entitled to (tailored to meet her needs *and* the needs of her family) and a set of goals for your child. The goal of the IFSP is to have parents involved in therapy for their children.

Birth to 3 programs cover lots of different services for children who have speech and language delays or hearing loss. Remember Marlowe, the young child who was born with hearing loss whom we introduced in Chapter 1? Her hearing aids were covered by her local EI program. Other kids can receive several hours of free or low-cost speech therapy a week. Sometimes, kids get multiple kinds of services, like speech therapy, physical therapy, and occupational therapy, too.

DR. MICHELLE'S TAKEAWAY

MAKE SURE YOUR child's IFSP lays out clear goals and involves all her caregivers in helping her achieve them.

PRESCHOOL SERVICES (AGES 3 TO 5)

Now, let's say your child is three years old and you or your child's daycare teacher is worried about how she's putting words together to communicate. Or she has already received services through Early Intervention and you want her to keep getting them. **Preschool Special Education** is the name for federally mandated services for children ages 3 to 5 who need some extra help. Sometimes, services for kids this age are referred to as **Section 619 services**, named after the section of the IDEA law that establishes them. Different states and cities may also have their own names for the committees and offices that evaluate preschool kids and help families get services.

Your child is entitled to free special services at this age—provided she meets your state's criteria—even if she does not attend a preschool. If she's home with a parent, grandparent, or other full-time caregiver, she can get these services. If she goes to a private daycare or preschool, including religious and parochial schools, she can get them, too. Just as with Early Intervention, a teacher or medical professional can also recommend your child get evaluated for services.

If your child qualifies for services, he will receive what's known as an **Individualized Education Program**, or **IEP**. You will hear this term so often over the next year (or longer) that you'll be surprised when other parents don't know it! An IEP is a legal document that spells out what diagnosis your child has received and what services she will get. Your child's IEP will state your child's current level of functioning and include goals for her to achieve.

Depending on her needs, your child can get lots of different kinds of services. She may get a free preschool education at a specialized school, like a local school for kids with communication difficulties. She might get transportation to the school paid for. She may receive a few hours of speech therapy at a speech therapist's office each week. Or she may have an extra teacher in the classroom to help her out.

The IDEA lists 13 categories of disabilities—remember, that's the term the law uses—that can qualify children ages 3 through 21 for services. (Some states also use an extra, optional category, called **developmental delays**, for kids ages 3 to 9.) **Many of the difficulties, delays, and disorders that we've discussed in this book fall under several of these IDEA categories**, including:

- ○ Speech or language impairment
- ○ Deafness
- ○ Hearing impairment
- ○ Autism
- ○ Specific learning disability

━━━━ DR. MICHELLE'S TAKEAWAY ━━━━

IT'S IMPORTANT TO look into preschool services for your child if you suspect she has delays. Remember that she is gearing up for elementary school, and the sooner you address any difficulties and get her support, the better.

SCHOOL-AGE SERVICES (AGE 5 AND OLDER)

Your child is ready for kindergarten and he still has difficulty pronouncing lots of common speech sounds, or he's stuck in a reading rut in first grade, or he's in second grade and his teacher thinks he might have learning and attention deficits. Now what?

Welcome to the special education process. **Your child can receive free special education services if he attends a public or private school or if he is homeschooled. The IDEA says he is entitled to receive a free and appropriate public education in the least restrictive environment.** But there's a catch: The law doesn't always make it easy—and neither do schools—to get those services.

To qualify, your child must, according to the IDEA, have a recognized disability (again, that's the word the law uses) and this disability must adversely affect his academic performance. **So not every kid who faces challenges is going to meet this threshold.** In Dr. Michelle's opinion, **these standards often mean that kids who need help do not qualify for it until they are too far behind.**

Your child will receive an evaluation to see if he qualifies for an IEP. If your child attends public school, the IEP process will typically happen at his school. Social workers and administrators at the school should help guide you through the evaluation process. If your child goes to a private or parochial school or is homeschooled, her evaluation will take place through your local school district; you may have to bring her to an office or public school to receive the evaluation.

PARENTING TIP

IF YOUR CHILD doesn't qualify for services through his school one year, try again the next year. A child's challenges and needs can change over time. Often, having your child's teacher aware of how his difficulties are affecting him can help in the evaluation process. Keep trying to get help through your school, and don't let one rejection bring you down.

If your child qualifies for services, his IEP will specify the services he is entitled to. It will set out specific, measurable goals. The word *individualized* in IEP is there for a reason: Every parent and child's IEP experience is going to be different, depending on the challenges your child has, his age, and his school environment. For many families, the IEP process is fraught with bureaucracy; for others, it is relatively easy and painless. There are *lots* of rules that govern the IEP process, everything from the duration of time it should take to get an evaluation to when your child's IEP should be renewed. These rules, while important for maintaining the integrity of the process, can also make it hard for parents to get help for their child. The IDEA contains important safeguards for parents who are unhappy with the process. It allows them to ask for independent evaluations, request a hearing to address their grievances, or set up a dispute-resolution process. Consult the Resources section at the end of this chapter for some of Dr. Michelle's favorite websites to help you familiarize yourself with the relevant laws and terminology and to find a description of the safeguards available to parents.

Nearly 6 million students ages 6 to 17 across the United States received services under the IDEA in 2013, according to a U.S. Department of Education report to Congress published in 2015. The most common reason was for having a specific learning disability; the second most common reason was for speech and language impairment. **For kids with communication challenges, special education can take many forms.** Remember that speech and language difficulties can intersect, and that speech and language issues can often co-occur with behavioral and academic issues that can make learning difficult. Here are some common forms of intervention, also called **service delivery models**, that your elementary school–age child may receive for a broad array of communication issues:

○ **Related services** refer to when a child receives educational instruction from a **general education** (or regular) classroom, but receives additional help, such as speech therapy, occupational therapy, physical therapy, or reading instruction. Speech therapy provided as a related service could take place either in a small group or in a one-on-one setting. It can also take place at school, in the classroom, or at a separate location.

○ An **inclusion classroom,** also sometimes called an **integrated classroom,** refers to a classroom that has a mixture of kids—some with IEPs who may have speech, language, or learning disabilities and who require specialized instruction to succeed in the classroom, as well as some kids who are typically developing. In such situations, two teachers—a general education teacher and a special education teacher— work together to help all the children in the classroom learn the material.

○ A **self-contained classroom** is composed solely of kids who have special learning needs. For these kids, a general education classroom or integrated classroom does not meet their educational needs. Self-contained classrooms may be taught by speech and language therapists (who also hold a teaching certification) or special education teachers.

━━━━━━━━ **PARENTING TIP** ━━━━━━━━

IF YOUR CHILD qualifies for services, work hard to schedule her extra help during a time of the day that she learns best. Sometimes schools offer extra help after school, but that's precisely the time when lots of kids are tired and burned out from learning. Make sure your child gets the services when she will most benefit from them.

Some schools or districts go beyond federal standards and provide services to a wide range of kids; count yourself lucky if that's the case for you. In addition, school-age children with communication difficulties can sometimes get extra help under a federal law called the **Rehabilitation Act of 1973**, which calls for accommodations for children with disabilities. Often called **504 plans**, after the section of the law that governs them, these accommodations can include extra classroom teachers for children with special learning challenges. See the Resources section for a guide to finding out more about 504 plans.

━━━━━━━━ **DR. MICHELLE'S TAKEAWAY** ━━━━━━━━

GETTING HELP FOR your child can be complicated and time-consuming. Don't be shy: Ask for help from your child's teacher and school, and keep advocating for your child.

PRIVATE OPTIONS FOR GETTING HELP FOR YOUR CHILD

As we've explained, not every child is eligible for all those free or low-cost public speech language therapy (or other therapy) services. If you go through the evaluation process by way of your local school and your child doesn't qualify, but still shows delays in speech or language skills that you think are affecting his communication, social, or academic skills, **Dr. Michelle strongly suggests you pursue speech language therapy using another route**. Or, your family may want to start with alternative options to begin with, knowing some of the roadblocks often involved in gaining free services.

To receive services in settings outside of your local school district, your child must go through an evaluation process, just as for publicly available interventions, but you will likely have to pay for this evaluation. Depending on your health insurance, you may be able to get reimbursed for the cost. **But the threshold for qualifying for these services can be different** when compared with the public sphere. Private practitioners who aren't bound to strict government or school district standards are likely to happily provide services to kids who face challenges because they recognize that many kids will benefit from extra help.

Let's outline three options you might want to consider for your child, along with some of their pros and cons.

PRIVATE PRACTITIONERS

Private practitioners are specialists who work out of an office or make home visits. Some may accept medical insurance or they can provide you with an invoice that has **ICD-10 codes** (universal codes for medical billing), which can be submitted to your insurer to get reimbursement. See the Resources section of this chapter to find a therapist in your area.

Among the upsides of working with a private practitioner:

○ Your child will receive high-quality, individualized therapy in a 1:1 setting in your home or in a location that is convenient for you.
○ You or a caregiver can be more involved and communicative with the therapist than in a school setting because you or

another caregiver will usually be present for therapy sessions, or you'll be around to meet with the therapist before or after the session.

○ Private practitioners typically work year-round, so your child's therapy does not stop during school breaks.

Among the downsides:

○ You may be paying a lot of money if your health insurance does not cover these services.
○ You have to take your child to therapy, and travel time can add up.
○ Scheduling the best appointment slot can be challenging if your child has other commitments, like sports or music lessons.

HOSPITAL (OUTPATIENT) CLINICS

Some hospitals have outpatient clinics that specialize in speech, language, and hearing evaluations and treatment. These clinics typically accept many types of medical insurance.

Among the upsides of hospital clinics are:

○ You will likely receive high-quality, individualized therapy for your child that is affordable.
○ You can be involved in your child's treatment because you can be at the clinic with him when therapy takes place.
○ Some hospitals may have access to extra resources, like sound-treated rooms or ear-nose-throat doctors (ENTs) on staff.

Among the downsides:

○ You will have to bring your child to another location for this therapy, and the time that you are able to schedule his sessions may not be ideal (such as after school hours).

○ If your child is struggling in school, it may be hard for a therapist from an outside clinic to communicate with his teachers about specific difficulties and strategies to use in the classroom.

COLLEGE AND UNIVERSITY CLINICS

Colleges and universities that have undergraduate and graduate programs in Speech-Language Pathology usually have speech, language, and hearing clinics on or close to campus. Under the supervision of licensed and certified therapists, graduate students work with children experiencing difficulties. Payment for services is affordable and often on a sliding scale. Some may also accept medical insurance.

Among the upsides of college and university clinics:

○ You can likely get very affordable services for your child.
○ The individual helping your child is likely steeped in some of the latest research in the field.
○ Students working in clinics are often enthusiastic about their new profession and strive to help young children.

Among the downsides:

○ Unlike a veteran practitioner, students helping your child will not have decades of experience treating kids (although their supervisor will), and these individuals may rotate on a regular basis.
○ As with other private practitioners, you will have to bring your child to therapy, and travel time can add up.
○ Clinics often have lengthy breaks due to the academic schedule that may not overlap with your child's school or daycare schedule.

A PARENT'S PERSPECTIVE

Joshua's Story

When Joshua was about three years old, his mom noticed that he didn't seem to be producing speech sounds like other children did. Through the local daycare that he attended, his mom contacted a local social worker in the town in southern Virginia where the family lived. The social worker said Joshua was too young to receive services because he had a good grasp of spoken language. But as he got older, his mom felt that his articulation wasn't improving, so she took him to a local hospital clinic to receive speech services, which she paid for herself. "It started to hit the pocket," she said. She then successfully petitioned her local public school system to provide speech therapy services for her son. Joshua attended a private preschool and was approved for an IEP. Even as he progressed through the early elementary school years, attending both public and private schools, Joshua still struggled to pronounce his speech sounds and received speech language therapy. One of the things his mother liked best was that some of the therapists gave him homework, assigning Joshua to practice specific words at home that were hard for him, like *gorilla*.

It took many years for Joshua to successfully pronounce tricky sounds like his *r* correctly, but his mom credits many hours of speech therapy practice with helping him. "It's been such a noticeable difference," she said. "He is conscious of how he speaks in conversation."

LET'S LOOK AT METHODS OF SPEECH LANGUAGE THERAPY

First we got you through an evaluation. Now it's time to focus on what happens once therapy begins.

No matter how you decide to pursue help for your infant, toddler, or school-age child, Dr. Michelle urges you to be aware of some basic professional guidelines for speech language therapy. The speech language therapist should be using **evidence-based practice** when working with you and your child. Evidence-based practice is a general term used in many different clinical practices that asks practitioners to take a multifactor approach in evaluating and treating patients. In 2005, ASHA published guidelines for evidence-based practices urging speech language therapists to consider three important factors when working with clients:

1. Speech language therapists should use **research-based evidence** when making decisions about evaluation and treatment. This means that your child's therapy should be based on academic research stating its effectiveness rather than simply on anecdotes and personal likes and dislikes.

2. The family's **unique perspective**, including preferences, cultural considerations, and values, are to be taken into account in the provision of the child's services. If your child is struggling to say words, your therapist may start with the names of family members or the name of a pet. If your child lives in an urban environment, he might want to learn words that are relevant to his neighborhood, like *bus* or *sidewalk*; names of farm animals are less important.

3. The speech language therapist should use her **expertise**, past experiences, and knowledge in the development of an appropriate and unique therapy plan for your child.

These three guidelines have been established as the gold standard for speech language therapists when working with clients. Dr. Michelle strongly urges parents to make sure that any therapy your child receives contains these elements.

The therapist you engage will develop an individualized therapy plan to address your child's specific strengths and weaknesses. Think of therapy as climbing a ladder: When your child is first evaluated, the therapist will determine what rung of the ladder your child is on. The therapist will then come up with a plan that will contain long-term goals—which you can think of as the top of the ladder—such as improving the child's ability to be understood by others. The plan will also contain short-term goals—which you can think of as the rungs on the ladder—which are the incremental improvements needed to achieve the overall goal and to get to the top of the ladder.

And whatever the goals are, **speech language therapy should be enjoyable, because kids learn best when they are playing and having fun.** For toddlers, speech therapy may look very similar to play, but the therapist will structure the play to address both your child's long-term and short-term goals. For older children, therapy should still be enjoyable and individualized; the therapist should try to involve your child's particular interests, such as working on getting him talking about outer space, superheroes, or a favorite movie, to make the therapy session personalized and focused.

Speech language therapy is most effective if everyone integrally involved in your child's life is involved and on board. Make sure to reinforce at home what your child works on during therapy sessions. Start by setting up regular communication with your child's therapist(s). We know you're busy, and we know the professionals helping your child are, too, but a weekly note or progress report from the therapist tucked in your child's backpack, or a text message or email containing information about what can help you implement your child's therapy at home, can go a long way toward helping your child improve.

Now, Dr. Michelle will have you step into her virtual office and tell you about how speech language therapy actually works.

DIRECT SERVICES

Speech language therapy can involve either direct services or indirect services. With direct services, the therapist works with your child in a one-to-one, small group, or large group setting. Direct services can involve different types of activities; some of these are structured and others are unstructured. For example, **drill activities** are very structured and involve saying or repeating a sound, word, or phrase many times. For kids, these types of activities may be necessary to learn how to say a speech sound a new way, to learn how to put three words together to make a sentence, or to decode simple words.

Unstructured activities, sometimes called **play-based therapy**, or learning while engaged in play, involve taking the child's lead to practice communication skills. Play-based therapy takes place in a naturalistic environment—comfortable, familiar settings, such as at home while the child is participating in everyday activities like playing with toy trains. A technique that speech language therapists use during play-based therapy to increase a child's language skills is called **expansions**, where the therapist rephrases a child's utterance to be more complex. Let's say a three-year-old is playing with a toy farm and remarks, *Cow eat.* The therapist may reply, *The cow is eating grass,* in order to model an appropriate sentence and in hopes that the child will repeat the longer sentence. For some children, in particular babies and preschool-age children, unstructured play-based therapy may be best because it teaches new skills and reinforces these skills in a naturalistic environment. Other kids may respond best to a combination of structured and unstructured methods.

Speech language therapy may also involve teaching children to use **alternative and augmentative communication (AAC)** strategies to communicate. AAC refers to the process of using all forms of communication—other than speech—to express ideas, including using facial expressions, pointing, and symbols or pictures. AAC strategies can be high-tech or low-tech. Children with severe speech and language disabilities, including children who are nonverbal or have very few words for their age, may use AAC to either supplement oral communication or to replace it if they are not able to use speech.

AAC can involve using manual languages such as sign language, a picture board, or high-tech communication devices that have voice output. Tools can range from very small and simple yes/no pictures to large and complex devices such as a handheld computer or tablet with specialized software. Research shows that using AAC strategies and devices can supplement as well as facilitate speech production; AAC devices can sometimes even improve the speech of children with severe delays.

INDIRECT SERVICES

Speech language therapy can also be delivered through indirect services where the therapist provides consultation and training to family members or caregivers on how to improve a child's communication. One example of an indirect therapy approach to improve language in young children (birth to age 5) who have language delays is called *It Takes Two to Talk—The Hanen Program for Parents of Children with Language Delays.* This program was developed by researchers in Toronto, Canada, to educate and train parents of young children with language delays about how to interact with their children to improve their language and communication. Researchers have shown that this program, when done with the appropriate supervision of a therapist, can be effective.

DR. MICHELLE'S TRIED-AND-TRUE THERAPY TIPS AND STRATEGIES

Throughout this book, and especially in Chapter 7, we've discussed a lot of concerns that parents have when it comes to their child's speech, language, and hearing development. No two kids are alike— so no therapy session or strategy will be, either. Here are some tips from Dr. Michelle on what to look out for when your child receives therapy for some of the most common diagnoses:

○ **Apraxia:** Expect therapy for your child several times a week, with practice focusing on using all the speech sounds correctly in syllables, words, and sentences. Push hard for intensive therapy if you are seeking school-based services. However, remember from Chapter 2 that current scientific research does not support therapies that focus on mouth movements, such as blowing a horn, puckering, and drinking from a straw, which are sometimes used during therapy sessions for kids with apraxia but are not shown to improve the ability to make certain speech sounds.

○ **Social communication disorder:** Your child will likely work hard, over a period of many years, to understand the conventions of language, including practicing communicating with peers, adults, and teachers. Therapy may be most effective if your child is paired with a peer to practice his social language skills.

○ **Autism:** If your child is diagnosed with autism spectrum disorder, he should be working not only with a psychologist, special educator, and occupational therapist, but with a speech language therapist as well. Make sure that all specialists try to reinforce what he is practicing in speech language therapy. For example, if he is working on using gestures to communicate, show the OT and psychologist these gestures so that he can use them during sessions with those professionals, too.

○ **Dysarthria:** Your child will likely work with a physical therapist, occupational therapist, and speech language therapist, because his underlying challenge is a difficulty based in motor movements. Work with your child's speech language therapist to come up with ways for everyone involved in your child's life to communicate effectively with him.

○ **Language-based learning disability:** Your child will likely work specifically with teachers trained to help her with a particular learning issue. Be sure that your child's special education teachers are familiar with all of her language development history, even reaching back to the toddler years.

For a little more detail about what frequently goes on during therapy sessions, Dr. Michelle offers composite profiles of three children with some of the most commonly occurring challenges, based on some of her patients, and explains the strategies she would use to work with them.

Spencer is five and a half years old and has an articulation disorder. He doesn't say certain speech sounds correctly, and his family, teachers, and peers are having a hard time understanding him when he says words containing the sounds *s*, *z*, *sh*, *th*, *l*, and *r*.

Dr. Michelle would approach therapy for Spencer by concentrating on improving **speech production skills**—the coordination of respiration, phonation, and articulation. This therapy should improve his **speech intelligibility,** or his ability to be understood by others.

First, it's important for children to hear the difference between speech sounds in order to say them correctly, so Dr. Michelle frequently does something called **perceptual** or **ear training**. This involves listening for target sounds and hearing the difference between correct and incorrect productions. She would work with Spencer to help him hear the difference between the *s* and *sh* sounds. The *s* sound is particularly important, because the first sound in his name contains an *s* blend—an *s* plus another sound (in Spencer's case, *p*).

Next, Dr. Michelle would work with Spencer to practice saying his speech sounds correctly, placing his articulators—his tongue and lips—in the correct position to say these speech sounds alone and in words and sentences. The most important aspect of treatment for speech sound disorders is practice, practice, practice. Practice does make perfect when it comes to speech sound production, and it should take place during therapy, at home, and at school. This means it's important for Dr. Michelle to establish a communication system with Spencer's family and teachers so that everyone is able to help him succeed.

Sarah is an eight-year-old with auditory processing disorder (APD). She has difficulty following along in the classroom, especially when it is noisy or when the teacher walks around the room. An audiologist has confirmed that Sarah has auditory processing disorder, a hearing disorder that we discussed in Chapter 7, and that she needs to work with a speech language therapist to help her follow directions and process information better.

Dr. Michelle would approach therapy for Sarah by working with her classroom teacher on strategies, techniques, and adjustments to her routines that would improve Sarah's ability to understand auditory messages. Some activities that Dr. Michelle would use include **auditory training**, focusing on improving listening in situations where Sarah demonstrates deficits, such as in noisy environments. One way to do this is to have Sarah listen to quiet background noise while she's engaged in schoolwork and practice blocking out the noise while completing her task.

Dr. Michelle may also teach Sarah **compensation strategies**, skills that can be used in conjunction with listening, in order to understand the message. Examples of compensation strategies include paying attention to facial expressions and gestures, and relying on **context clues**—that is, using known words or phrases to figure out unknown or missed words. These strategies will help Sarah to understand the message that's been transmitted.

Dr. Michelle would also work with an audiologist to provide Sarah with an assistive listening device such as an FM unit. This device would help her at school by picking up her teachers' words through a microphone and sending them through FM radio waves directly to headphones Sarah would be wearing. The device would help Sarah hear her teachers better because it would reduce background noise.

DR. MICHELLE'S TAKEAWAY

FOR KIDS WITH APD, both direct and indirect services are often essential to achieve academic success.

Sam is a three-year-old with a language disorder. He uses only five words to communicate. Sam can understand language, follow directions, and point to objects, pictures, body parts, and clothing items, but he can become very frustrated when he is not able to express himself using words.

Dr. Michelle would approach therapy for Sam by working with him and his family to improve his expressive communication skills. Because Sam is young, he is likely to respond to play-based therapy, which means he would learn to say new words and use these new words while engaged in play activities. So, while playing with Sam with a play kitchen, Dr. Michelle would say new words that are important to him—words related to the play kitchen set that are also in Sam's home, like *spoon, bowl, milk, pour,* and *apple*.

To get Sam to say new words, Dr. Michelle would use various techniques such as **modeling**, in which a therapist says and repeats new words, as well as **imitating**, in which a therapist, typically through play, asks the child to say the new word. Dr. Michelle might also ask Sam questions that will elicit the new word from him, such as, *Do you want milk or an apple?* She might also manipulate Sam's play environment to encourage him to use a new word, saying, *Sam, you can stir the food now,* making sure the spoon is visible but just out of Sam's reach. This would encourage him to say, *Spoon!*

Once Sam has acquired more words, Dr. Michelle would use other strategies, such as expansions (mentioned earlier), in which the speech language therapist repeats what the child says and adds more words. So, if Sam said *milk* during playtime, the therapist would say *Sam pours milk* to encourage Sam to repeat those words. Dr. Michelle would also teach Sam's caregivers strategies to use to help him to improve his communication while he's working on acquiring new words, such as using gestures or signs for words that he was not yet able to say.

DR. MICHELLE'S TAKEAWAY

KIDS WITH EXPRESSIVE language delays should work with a speech language therapist to acquire new words. Expect a child with expressive language difficulties to need intervention throughout preschool and likely into elementary school.

COMMON QUESTIONS,

EXPERT ANSWERS

Dr. Michelle hears lots of questions from the parents of her patients, as well as parents at school pickup or on the playground, about the process for getting help. Here are some of the most common questions and her straightforward answers to help you find the best therapy situation for you and your child.

QUESTION: *How do I tell my child that he needs speech language therapy?*

ANSWER: Be open about what's going on, in an age-appropriate way. Toddlers or preschoolers may not realize they have speech or language difficulties. So, for a young child, it's okay to tell him that he is going to see Ms. X, and that he will play and talk with her. You can couch it as play, because that's just what it should be for a toddler or preschooler. Older children are likely to be more aware of their speech or language difficulties, so for a school-age child it's okay to tell him that he is going to work with a special teacher who will help him listen, speak, and talk to others. Remind him that *everybody* has something he needs to work on—even Mom and Dad and other grown-ups.

QUESTION: *The speech language therapist doesn't like me to be in the room during her sessions with my child. Is this good or bad?*

ANSWER: It can be good. Your presence may be distracting for both your child and the therapist, and your child may work best knowing you are not watching. But parents, caregivers, and teachers should be included in all aspects of speech language intervention. Be sure to work with your child's therapist to establish a communication system so that you know what activities you can do at home to reinforce activities in the therapy room.

QUESTION: *My child's school said a speech language therapist isn't available to help my child, but an occupational therapist will work with him. Is this okay?*

ANSWER: No. If your child has a speech or language disorder or delay, then *only* a speech language therapist is the best professional to help your child. Other professionals can be great at what they do, but your child's therapy needs to be handled by the right expert. Remember that IFSPs and IEPs are legal documents, and if your local system isn't providing services to meet your child's needs, you can pursue remedies to get the help your child needs.

QUESTION: *My child doesn't like going to speech language therapy. What should I do?*

ANSWER: Not every professional is the perfect match for your child, and vice versa. If your child is not happy to go to therapy (after a few weeks of getting acclimated), he likely won't improve. Try to work with your therapist to find strategies that work better for your child, and then consider shopping around for someone new. Don't be afraid to break up with your speech language therapist if you feel she is not a good match for your child.

RESOURCES

It can be very tricky, but extremely essential, of course, to navigate all the different aspects of getting the best help possible for your child. Here are some of the websites Dr. Michelle recommends to get the best information about where to find help, as well as how to get up-to-date information on the special education process.

- The University of North Carolina National Early Childhood Technical Assistance Center has a grant from the federal government to gather data and inform parents about the IDEA and the special education process: *http://ectacenter.org/*.
- To find out about your state's standards for eligibility for Early Intervention services, and to find state-specific websites for Early Intervention resources, check out this document from the National Early Childhood Technical Assistance Center: *http://www.nectac.org/~pdfs/topics/earlyid/partc_elig_table.pdf*.
- The National Center for Learning Disabilities has a great primer on the IDEA: *http://www.ncld.org/action-center/ learn-the-law*.
- Understood.org, a site devoted to helping educate parents about the special education process, has informative, accessible descriptions of different interventions, services, and special education law. In particular, we recommend these resources:

- An information sheet on preschool services: *https:// www.understood.org/en/learning-attention-issues/ treatments-approaches/early-intervention/how-section-619-can-help-your-preschooler.*
- An explanation of 504 plans and how they work: *https:// www.understood.org/en/school-learning/special-services/504-plan/understanding-504-plans.*
- A detailed account of the procedural safeguards available to parents under the IDEA, including an explanation of a dispute-resolution process: *https://www.understood.org/ en/school-learning/your-childs-rights/basics-about-childs-rights/important-safeguards-for-you-and-your-child.*

○ A qualified speech and language specialist can be found by going to the American Speech-Language-Hearing Association website at *www.asha.org* and clicking on Find a Professional.

INDEX